When
CRICKET *Was*
CRICKET

THE ASHES

In memory of Charles Ley and other departed *Mirror* photographers

© Haynes Publishing, 2013

The right of Adam Powley to be identified as the author of this Work has been asserted
by him in accordance with the Copyright, Designs & Patents Act 1988.

All rights reserved. No part of this publication may be reproduced, stored in a retrieval system
or transmitted, in any form or by any means, electronic, mechanical, photocopying, recording
or otherwise, without prior permission in writing from the publisher.

First published in 2013

A catalogue record for this book is available from the British Library

ISBN: 978-0-85733-188-5

Published by Haynes Publishing, Sparkford, Yeovil,
Somerset BA22 7JJ, UK
Tel: 01963 442030 Fax: 01963 440001
Int. tel: +44 1963 442030 Int. fax: +44 1963 440001
E-mail: sales@haynes.co.uk
Website: www.haynes.co.uk

Haynes North America Inc., 861 Lawrence Drive,
Newbury Park, California 91320, USA

Images © Mirrorpix

Creative Director: Kevin Gardner
Designed for Haynes by BrainWave

Printed and bound in the US

When
CRICKET *Was*
CRICKET

THE ASHES

A Nostalgic Look at a Century of the Greatest Rivalry

Adam Powley

Contents

RIGHT: A quartet of English veterans gathers at Edgbaston to witness the 1961 Test against Australia. Left to right: wicket-keeper Ernest "Tiger" Smith, who played with W G Grace; Sydney Barnes, who was ranked by the Aussies as the finest English bowler of the Edwardian era; Frank Woolley, one of the best-ever left-handers; and Wilfred Rhodes, the all-time great who played against the "enemy" at the ripe old age of 49.

Introduction

Sport, to a great extent, is built on its enduring rivalries. For all the understandable admiration for modern competition, with ultra-professional world-class talent playing in state-of-the-art stadiums, it is often the traditional, age-old contests that really matter. Two long-standing foes engaged in an unceasing battle for supremacy in famous old arenas provide an unrivalled sporting spectacle that captivates, enthrals and thrills like no other. And few of these compelling duels have such a rich heritage as cricket's Ashes series.

Ever since 1877, meetings between England and Australia have had a special appeal. The pitting of the British Empire's "mother country" against one of her colonies was always bound to stir something much more than mere sporting competitiveness. It is usually reduced to a valid but only partial perspective on the relationship: for the Aussies, cricket and the Ashes has provided an opportunity to express national identity and character, and the chance to get one over their stuffy former rulers; for the English it is a means to confirm deep-seated notions of power and prestige. It has, of course, been more complex and nuanced than this, but the frequent banter between "whingeing Poms" and chippy "convicts" underpins the fact that the Ashes is about much more than just cricket.

This book is a photographic portrait of this compelling rivalry. While it is based around a chronological recount of the various series for over a century, it is not an exhaustive encyclopedia, featuring detail on every ball, bat stroke and catch: sources such as the venerable *Wisden* and the superb cricinfo.com provide that and much, much more. Rather, it is a series of snapshots of the Ashes through time and across different places, featuring the scenes away from the action as much as the on-field activity itself.

Most of the photographs are, by necessity, of matches played in England. Newspapers would rarely send their own photographers halfway across the world at great cost (and where the strict control of expenses would, no doubt, be harder to enforce), but the summer matches with Australian touring teams became essential events that were covered in depth. The focus of this book, therefore, is on Ashes series in England.

Together, the pictures tell a vivid story, not just of the bare outcomes of match results and how series were decided (fascinating as they may be) but the whole sense of cricket's continuity and gradual change. The fading away of former heroes, the promise of new young talents, developments in how the game has been played, the almost imperceptible changes in the look of cricket grounds and the crowds that have filled them through the decades – the Ashes isn't just a story about cricket or even a sport, but about the history of two countries and their peoples. Here are just some of the wonderful images that illustrate that rich and magnificent heritage.

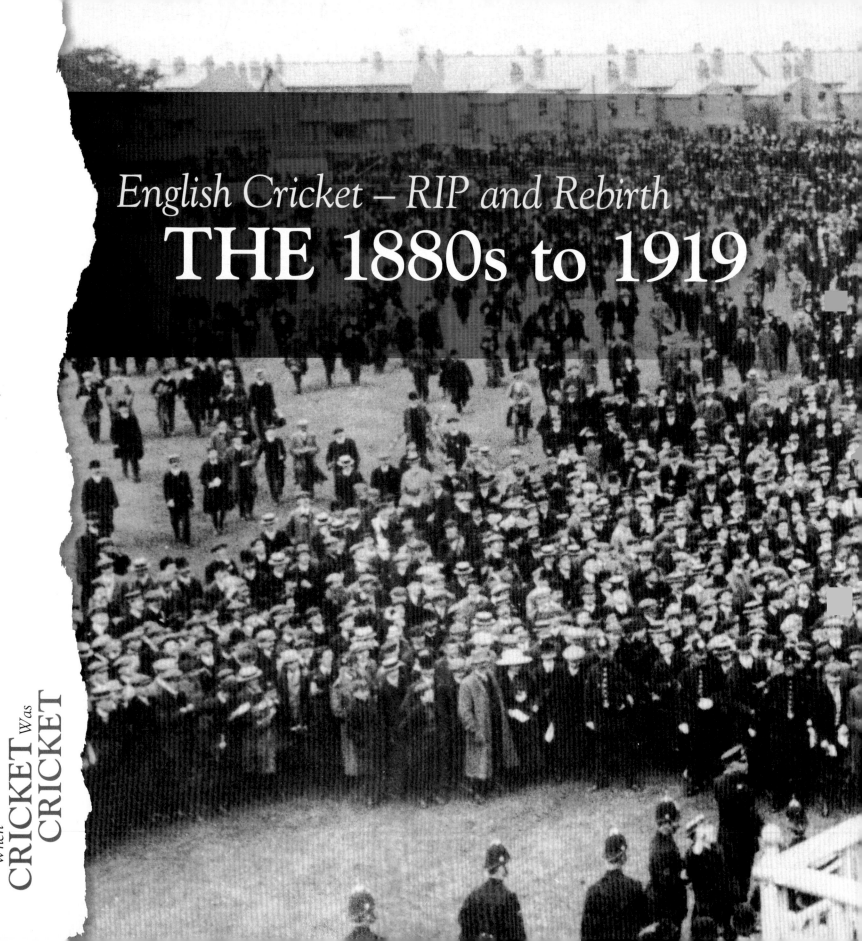

English Cricket – RIP and Rebirth
THE 1880s to 1919

On the final day of the first Test at Edgbaston in May 1909, the crowd surged onto the field to acclaim a memorable England victory. Any triumphalism engendered by the 10-wicket victory was short-lived however. The visitors rallied and won the next two Tests to take the series 2-1.

Matches between teams of cricketers that loosely played "for" England and Australia had taken place over a number of years in the latter half of the 19th century. A group of Aborigines arrived in England in 1868, played at over 40 grounds around the country, including Lord's, and drew huge crowds.

What is recognized as the first Test match between Australia and England was played in 1877, even if the term "Test" was not in usage at the time. The teams were made up of professionals – which meant the likes of W G Grace were absent – and, as such, were not regarded as pre-eminent line-ups in an era when the "Gentlemen Amateur" carried greater heft than his professional counterpart.

The Ashes proper arose from the third Australian touring party, which beat the England team (now including W G Grace) in 1882. The seven-run win, underpinned by "The Demon" Fred Spofforth's blistering 14 wickets for just 90 runs, was a humbling defeat for England on home turf and prompted much soul-searching among cricket lovers and the press – to the extent that a mock obituary in the *Sporting Times*, written by Reginald Shirley Brooks, appeared, "in affectionate remembrance of English cricket, which died at The Oval on 29th August, 1882. The body will be cremated and the ashes taken to Australia."

The following tour, in 1882–83, saw England re-establish primacy with a 2-1 series win, and led to the presentation of a tiny urn that, it is believed, contained the ashes of a burned bail. With honour salvaged, England went on to win a further seven consecutive series, though not without controversy. The Aussies refused to play in one match in the 1884–85 series over a payment dispute, and there was a brawl in the first match.

The 1891–92 series finally saw the Australians victorious again, but it was only fleeting, as England won the next three series, with Grace captaining the side in 1896. The Australians then enjoyed a period of ascendancy, winning four series on the spin. By 1903–04, the England team was organized under the auspices of the Marylebone Cricket Club (MCC), giving the official seal of approval to a side that had previously been run on a largely ad hoc commercial basis. The Ashes legend by that time had waned, and it was England captain Pelham Warner who did much to revive and establish the contest's mythic status. In 1905 Bernard Bosanquet, inventor of the "googly" (and father of the newsreader Reginald) mentioned "The Ashes" in an article in *Wisden*. During cricket's pre-war "golden age", the Ashes enjoyed a similarly gilded era, until the First World War intervened.

The madding Ashes crowd: Edwardian cricket fans at Edgbaston in 1909.

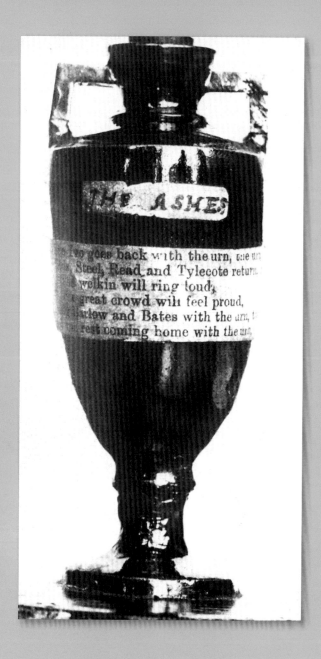

"Little urn" – the diminutive trophy that lies at the heart of the great England v Australia rivalry. The inscription, naming the leading players of the time, reads:

When Ivo goes back with the urn, the urn;
Studds, Steel, Read and Tylecote return, return;
The welkin will ring loud,
The great crowd will feel proud,
Seeing Barlow and Bates with the urn, the urn;
And the rest coming home with the urn.

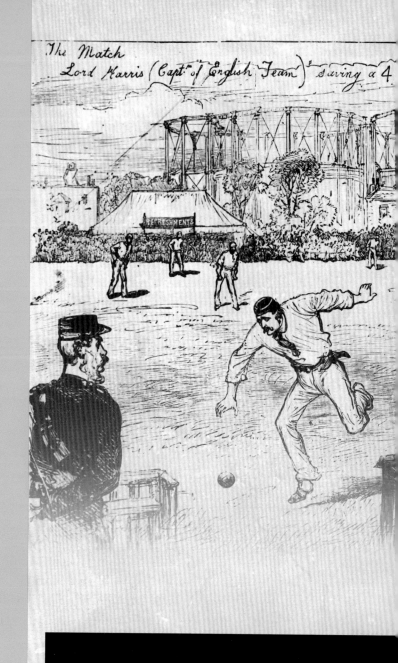

ABOVE: An illustration of the 1880 Test against Australia at The Oval, showing Lord Harris saving a four.

LEFT: The Australian touring side of 1884. Seated right, in the front row, is Fred Spofforth, "The Demon" fast bowler whose exploits with the ball were so influential in the origins of the Ashes.

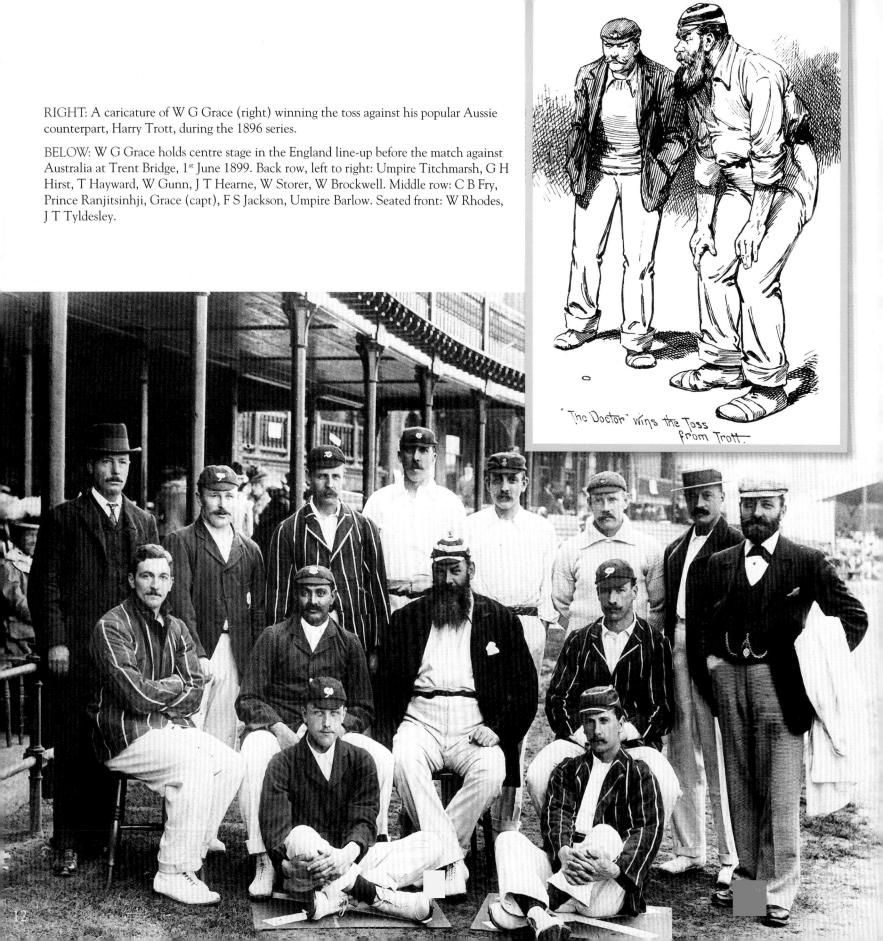

RIGHT: A caricature of W G Grace (right) winning the toss against his popular Aussie counterpart, Harry Trott, during the 1896 series.

BELOW: W G Grace holds centre stage in the England line-up before the match against Australia at Trent Bridge, 1st June 1899. Back row, left to right: Umpire Titchmarsh, G H Hirst, T Hayward, W Gunn, J T Hearne, W Storer, W Brockwell. Middle row: C B Fry, Prince Ranjitsinhji, Grace (capt), F S Jackson, Umpire Barlow. Seated front: W Rhodes, J T Tyldesley.

"The Doctor" wins the Toss from Trott.

ABOVE: The Australian team of 1899. The series that year was notable for being W G Grace's last, and having knocks of 135 each for Victor Trumper and Clem Hill in a 10-wicket win at Lord's, and four draws, to leave the visitors the winners by a 1-0 margin.

THE AUSTRALIAN TEAM ENTERING THE CRICKET GROUN[D]
FOR THEIR FIRST MATCH, MAY 4th 190[ ]

THE NAMES ARE : 1. R. A. DUFF, 2. J. J. KELLY, 3. C. HILL. 4. A. COTTER, 5. W. W[ ]
7. A. J. HOPKINS, 8. V. TRUMPER, 9. C. E. MC LEOD, 10. M. A. NOBLE (VICE-CAPT[ ]

14

10 11 COPYRIGHT

RYSTAL PALACE,

1STRONG, 6. S. E. GRÉGORY,
11. J. DARLING (CAPTAIN).

LEFT: The 1905 tour began with a meeting between the tourists and "gentlemen of England" at Crystal Palace, on 4th May.

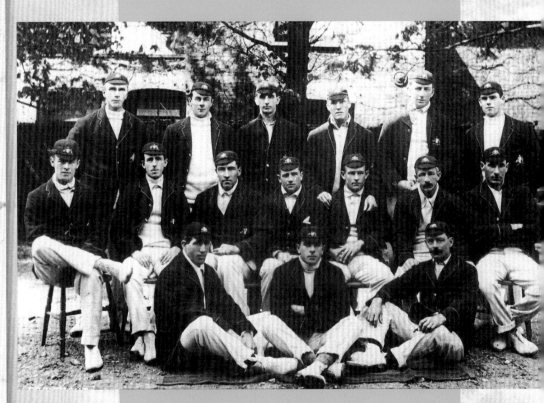

ABOVE: Resplendent in blazers and caps, the 1909 Australian side came through a wonderfully contested series to cling onto the Ashes, thanks to a 2-1 series win. Warren Bardsley (back row, second left) became the first cricketer to score two centuries in one match (136 and 130), registering his feat at The Oval.

By 1909, England were calling on new heroes to defend Ashes pride, and had an opening partnership ready for a new age. Walking out for the first Test at Edgbaston was an Oxbridge man, C B Fry (right), who had perfect Establishment credentials. He was also a captivating personality who repeatedly stood (unsuccessfully) for Parliament, a classicist and talented writer, and a prodigious all-round sportsman. Fry played for England and Southampton at football, and was an accomplished long jumper.

Jack Hobbs (left), by contrast, hailed from humble origins in Cambridge to become one of the great batsmen, and the only Englishman included in *Wisden*'s list of the greatest cricketers of the 20th century. As a brilliant but unshowy sportsman, he was a paragon of cricketing virtue for a generation of fans.

In the absence of an Ashes series in the immediate aftermath of the end of the First World War, the Australian Imperial Forces side toured England in 1919. At Leicester, the visitors got in some nets practice, which proved useful for captain H L Collins – he scored 121 in the drawn match.

Cricketers were the big stars of the era – more so than footballers – and attracted an ardent following wherever they went, as well as the attentions of the press. Few were as popular as C B Fry. He captained the England side to a 1-0 series win in 1912, and while by 1922 his Ashes career was firmly behind him, he could still draw a crowd, as on this visit to Brighton.

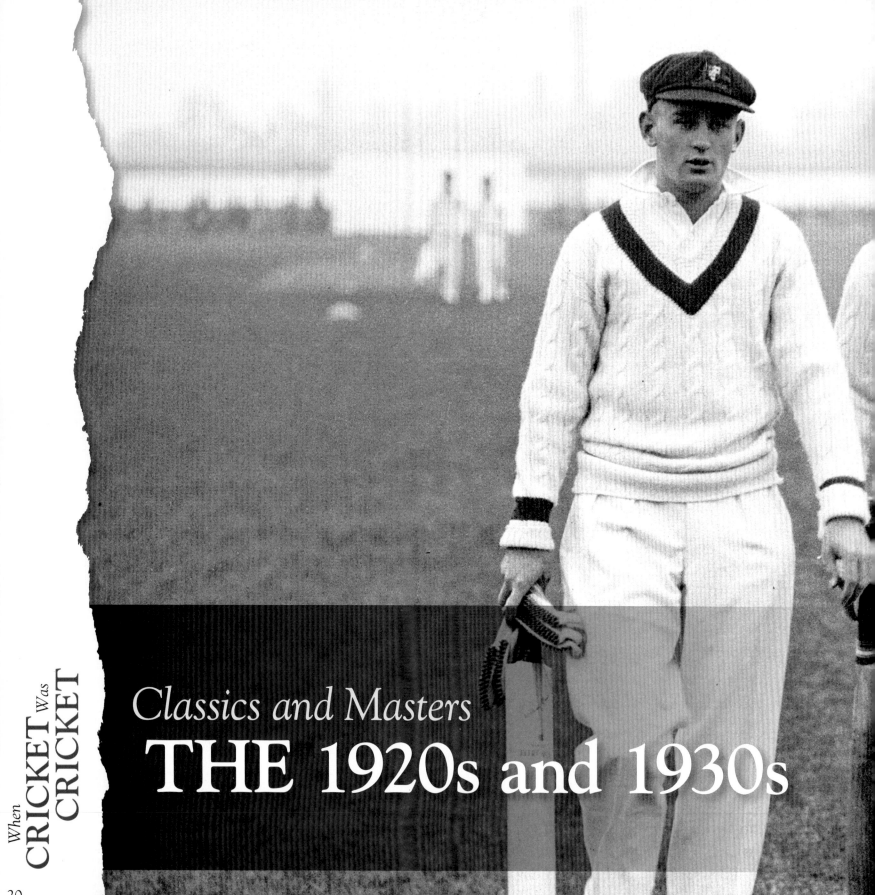

Classics and Masters
THE 1920s and 1930s

A triumvirate of Aussie tourists in a 1930 tour match at Leicester. Left to right: Stan McCabe, Clarrie Grimmett and Alec Hurwood. Grimmett was the New Zealand-born spinner who is said to have pioneered the "flipper". He twice took 10 wickets or more in an Ashes Test match (in 1924–25 and 1930). McCabe was a prolific batsman and the mainstay of the Aussie order, and could withstand even the most fierce pace attacks exemplified in his performance during the Bodyline series of 1932–33.

Resumption of Ashes contests after the First World War heralded a golden period for a very strong Australian side. Under the leadership of Warwick Armstrong, Australia inflicted the first ever five-match whitewash in Ashes history in 1920–21.

For the swift return in 1921, both sides travelled on the same ship, but if there was any advantage at seeing their opponents at close quarters, it was rendered meaningless by another heavy defeat for England. They did at least avoid another whitewash, thanks to a washed-out Old Trafford Test and a draw at The Oval.

Local radio coverage made its Test debut in the 1924–25 series and listeners were treated to another thumping Aussie victory. The home side piled on the runs and swiftly established a series-securing win, but, at least from England's view, the visitors stopped the rot with a win at the Melbourne Cricket Ground (MCG) – the first for England in 11 years. The kernel of a competitive England side, with Jack Hobbs, Herbert Sutcliffe and Maurice Tate to the fore, was emerging.

That promise was realized in 1926 when England won a rain-affected series 1-0, with the deciding Test in large part won by the bowling of 48-year-old Wilfred Rhodes, who had made his Ashes debut in the last year of the 19th century.

England then won the 1928–29 series by a handsome 4-1 margin, but the debut of the 20-year-old Aussie Donald Bradman hinted that any hope of English domination was to be short-lived. By 1930 "The Don" was on his remorseless path to becoming the greatest batsman of the 20th century, harvesting 974 runs as the Aussies won the series 2-1. Desperate times called for desperate measures, with notorious results in the 1932–33 "Bodyline" series (see page 40), but England's recovery of the urn was fleeting: Australia would hold precedence for six successive series, and with the intervention of the Second World War between 1939 and 1945, reign supreme for 19 years.

The 1934 series was notable for the absence of Douglas Jardine and the injured Harold Larwood, and the presence of BBC TV cameras for the first time. The 1938 Oval Test was the last Ashes encounter to be played under the "timeless" rules, whereby deciding rubbers would be played until there was a positive result or a tie.

Jack Hobbs in brief action at Trent Bridge in 1926. While the rain-dominated series opener meant only 32 runs were scored (all by England in just 50 minutes of play), Hobbs had a fine series, becoming the first cricketer to pass 4,000 Test runs.

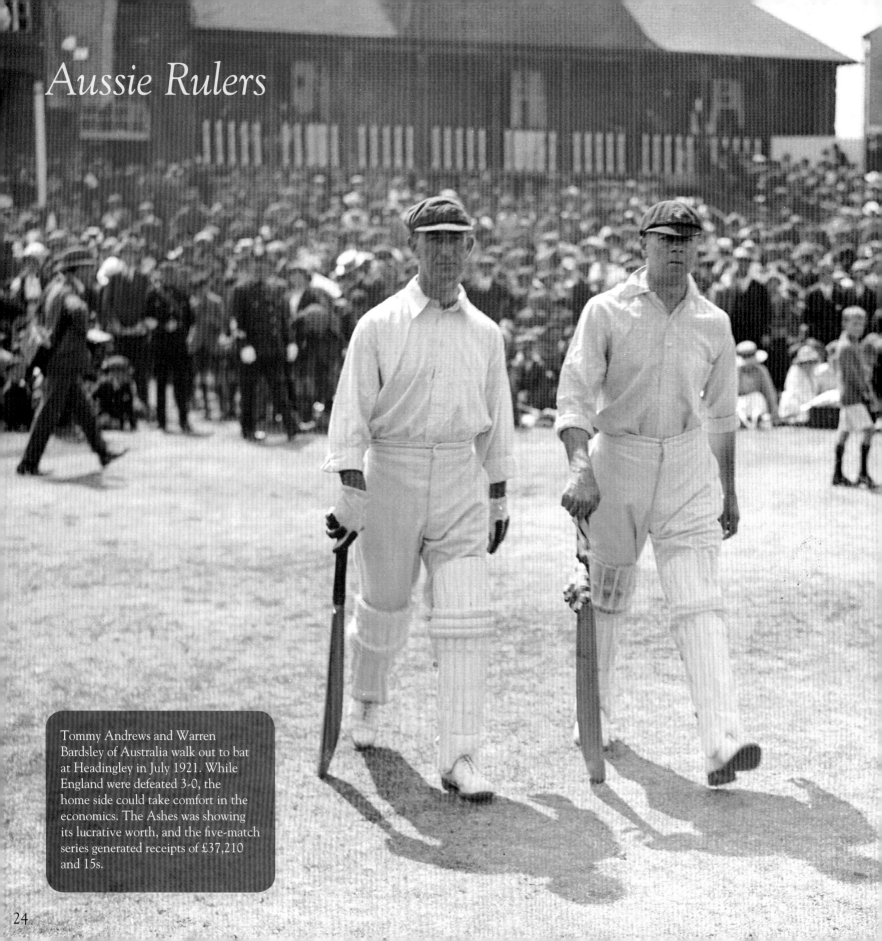

Aussie Rulers

Tommy Andrews and Warren Bardsley of Australia walk out to bat at Headingley in July 1921. While England were defeated 3-0, the home side could take comfort in the economics. The Ashes was showing its lucrative worth, and the five-match series generated receipts of £37,210 and 15s.

ABOVE: By 1926, Bardsley was partnered with Bill Woodfull. Woodfull was known as "The Rock" for his steadfast performances as both opening bat and as a skipper who displayed superb leadership.

RIGHT: Clarrie Grimmett grins and bears it for the cameras in 1925.

Elias "Patsy" Hendren takes to the field in the drawn Old Trafford Test of 1926. Hendren played for 14 years in Ashes matches and scored three centuries against the Aussies, albeit a small fraction of his total of 170 first-class tons.

LEFT: Hobbs and Sutcliffe formed an opening pair that could compete with Australia's frontline batsmen. They both notched centuries in the second innings of the final Test at The Oval – Sutcliffe with 161, Hobbs with a round 100 – to give England the advantage and what proved to be an eventual 289-run victory, which brought the Ashes back to England.

BELOW: Hobbs hit 12 centuries against Australia and notched the last at the age of 46, with 142 in Melbourne in March 1929, though he couldn't prevent the Aussies winning by five wickets.

Tours in the 1920s could last up to six months. In preparation for the Ashes series in 1928–29, England played Western Australia in Perth in October 1928, and drew a three-day game. Western Australia's Arthur Richardson caught Percy Chapman off Walter Evans' bowling – and Chapman was on his way to the pavilion before the ball was in Richardson's hands.

The 1928–29 series was one of England's most successful visits down under. Building on the narrow victory of 1926, the visitors had Wally Hammond to thank for his considerable part in gaining a 4-1 scoreline. While Hammond was not at his most prolific in the first Test at Brisbane – he was out for 44 after being caught by Bob Woodfull off bowler Jack Gregory (above) in the first innings – the record-setting 675 win set the tone for the series, and Hammond ended with an aggregate of 905 runs.

Many happy returns: during the interval when bad light stopped play on day two of the second Test at the Sydney Cricket Ground in 1928, Mr Alfred Noble presented a boomerang to Jack Hobbs for his 46th birthday.

Some of England's fielders were grounded as Australia advanced to 397 in the opening innings of the third Test at the MCG, but a double century from Wally Hammond and 135 from Sutcliffe in the second innings underpinned the tourists' three-wicket win and, with it, secured the Ashes.

ABOVE: Bert Oldfield pounced to attempt a stumping of George Duckworth in the 1929 fourth Test at the Adelaide Oval, a timeless Test that lasted seven days, with England winning by 12 runs.

34

England received a cordial welcome during the 1928–29 tour – but the reception would be distinctly different three years later.

ABOVE: The year 1930 was the one when Australia struck back and Don Bradman (second right, front row) made his indelible mark. Jack Hobbs was still producing the goods for England, but in a sure sign of the changing of the guard, Bradman's magnificent aggregate of 974 runs eclipsed Hobbs' Ashes swansong and aided his side towards a 2-1 series win.

LEFT: A well-turned-out Stan McCabe with tour treasurer T Howard in June 1930.

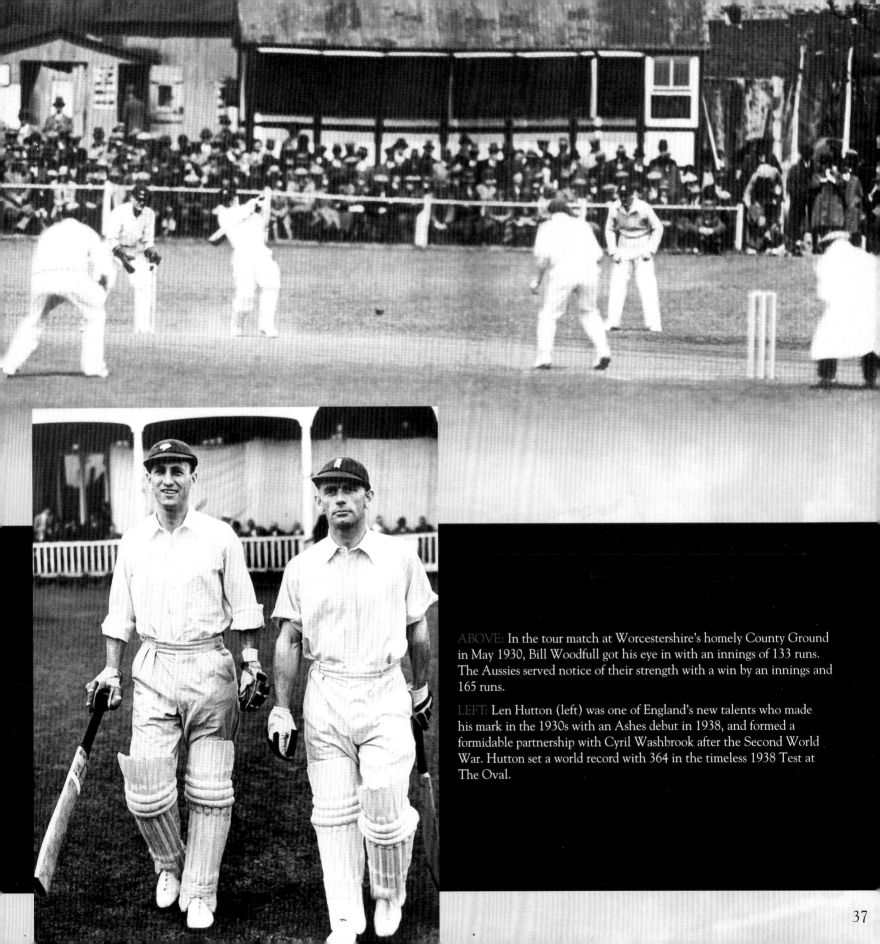

ABOVE: In the tour match at Worcestershire's homely County Ground in May 1930, Bill Woodfull got his eye in with an innings of 133 runs. The Aussies served notice of their strength with a win by an innings and 165 runs.

LEFT: Len Hutton (left) was one of England's new talents who made his mark in the 1930s with an Ashes debut in 1938, and formed a formidable partnership with Cyril Washbrook after the Second World War. Hutton set a world record with 364 in the timeless 1938 Test at The Oval.

37

The Don

In 20 years of Ashes history – between 1928 and 1948 – no batsman made such a defining impact as Don Bradman. Had war not interrupted this period of sustained excellence, Bradman's average may have been perfection. As it was, he set a standard that was a fraction under 90, a phenomenal achievement of consistency from the greatest batsman the world has seen.

Bradman made his debut as a 19-year-old in 1928 and contributed a high score of 112, but it was in 1930 that he truly announced his near unanswerable talent. Over the five Test series he garnered 974 runs for a record-setting average of 139.14. His style may not have entirely satisfied a handful of the most exacting of technical purists but his hungry pursuit of runs made him Australia's most potent weapon in what was a strong overall side.

So fundamental was his talent that England had to devise a new and cynical tactic – the Bodyline – to stem the flow of runs from Bradman's bat. Despite this, Bradman still plundered nearly 300 runs in the Bodyline series with an average of 56, and in subsequent series scored with almost monotonous predictability: 758 in 1934, 810 in 1936–37, and 19 centuries in all, finishing with a grand total of 5,028 runs culled from exasperated English bowlers.

The Don was a competitive adversary who relished taking on the old enemy. Test cricket is, of course, a team game, but the fact that Australia lost just one Ashes series while Bradman was at the crease illustrates his central role in the Aussies – all but monopolizing the crown for a generation.

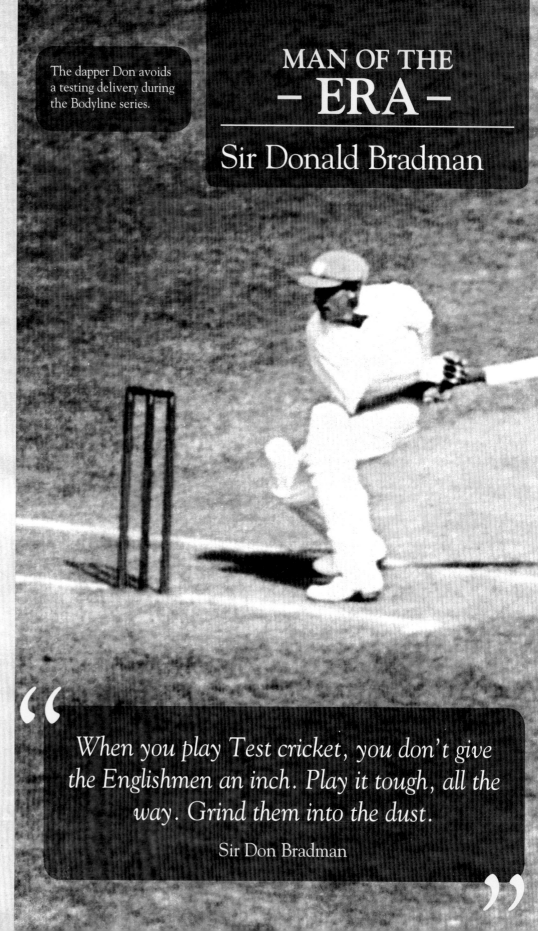

The dapper Don avoids a testing delivery during the Bodyline series.

MAN OF THE
– ERA –

Sir Donald Bradman

When you play Test cricket, you don't give the Englishmen an inch. Play it tough, all the way. Grind them into the dust.

Sir Don Bradman

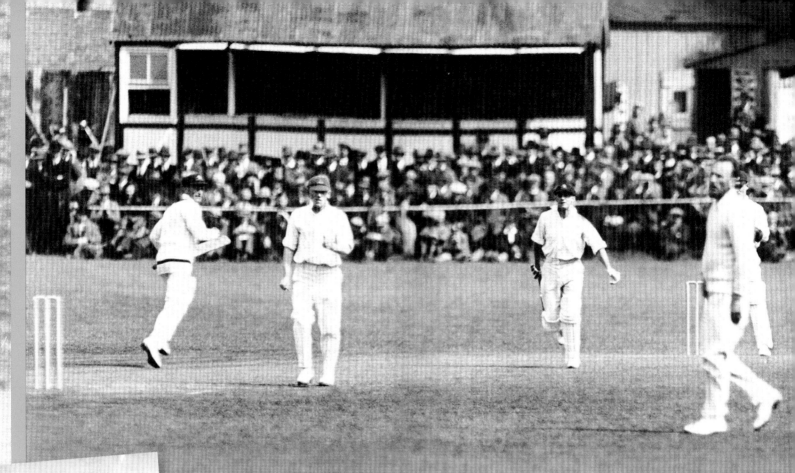

ASHES
— SCORECARD —

Sir Donald Bradman

Name: Donald Bradman

Born: 1908

Appearances: 37

High score: 334 (Headingley, 1930)

Batting average: 89.78

Best figures: 1-23 (Adelaide, 1933)

Bowling average: 51.00

ABOVE: Bradman doing what he did best: scoring runs against an English side, this time 236 against Worcestershire in 1930.

RIGHT: England's old nemesis arrives at Heathrow airport in 1974.

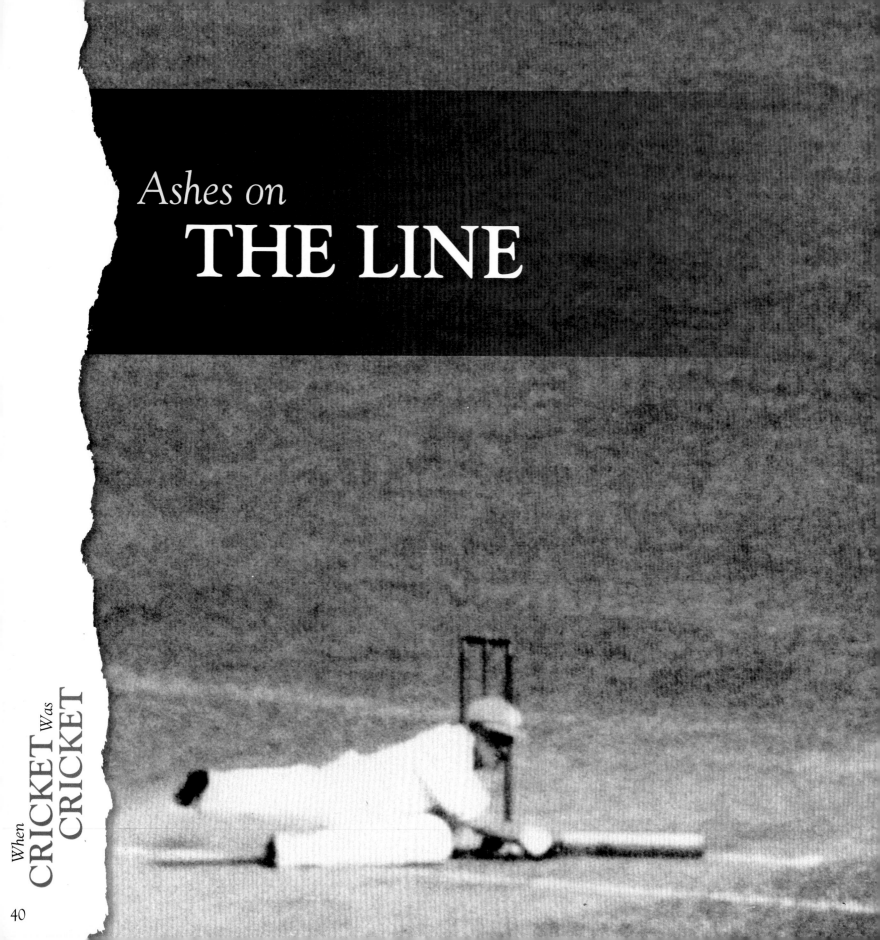

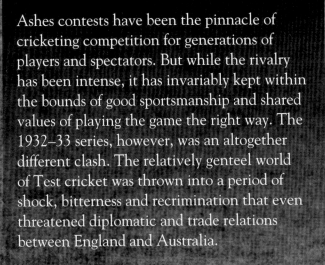

Ashes contests have been the pinnacle of cricketing competition for generations of players and spectators. But while the rivalry has been intense, it has invariably kept within the bounds of good sportsmanship and shared values of playing the game the right way. The 1932–33 series, however, was an altogether different clash. The relatively genteel world of Test cricket was thrown into a period of shock, bitterness and recrimination that even threatened diplomatic and trade relations between England and Australia.

> ## *"I'm afraid it was a slightly murky episode."*
>
> George "Gubby" Allen, speaking to the BBC

Don Bradman, the darling of Australian cricket, is forced to take desperate evasive action to avoid being struck by a ball from Bill Voce during the infamous Bodyline series of 1932–33.

The genesis of Bodyline stemmed from Don Bradman's domination of English bowlers in 1930. The Don's seeming impregnability threatened to derail any English attempts to win the Ashes before a ball had been bowled.

Douglas Jardine had other ideas. Named as captain in July 1932 for the MCC's tour of Australia, Jardine devised a strategy for dealing with Bradman and his colleagues. It hinged on a flaw Jardine believed he had identified in Bradman's technique, whereby he was vulnerable to short-pitched balls on the leg-side.

Employing a four-man pace attack, led by the lightning quick Harold Larwood, Jardine devised a more aggressive variation on "leg-theory" policy. Though he denied the specific intention, batsmen were targeted by swift, short deliveries, with an on-side field breathing down the batsman's neck to exploit any loose defensive shots. There were next to no fielders on the off-side, resulting in an intimidating, almost suffocating field that was actually outlawed in 1947. Jardine called it "fast leg theory", with his bowlers sending down short-pitched cannon shots at up to 90mph, which reared up into the batsmen's exposed body and head. The Aussies soon had another name for it – Bodyline.

LEFT: Douglas Jardine, captain of the MCC England cricket team in September 1932, with Captain O'Sullivan of the *SS Orantes*, en route to Australia.

Peevish, brusque and thin-skinned when it came to criticism and his view of opponents, Jardine was an Indian-born Oxford blue and amateur "gentleman" who resorted to the utmost professionalism to win cricket matches. Many Australians despised him for his supposed embodiment of the high-handed and mean-spirited nature of their country's colonial rulers. Merited or not, the loathing was mutual: Jardine made it his mission not just to beat the Australians but to rub their noses in it.

The MCC team in Barbados in 1930. Led by the Hon. F S Calthorpe (sixth from left), the side included just a handful of those who were to play in the Bodyline series: wicket-keeper Les Ames (far left), Bob Wyatt (to Calthorpe's right) and Bill Voce (last on right). Calthorpe would make way for Jardine, and, with this change, England's outlook took a more ruthless turn.

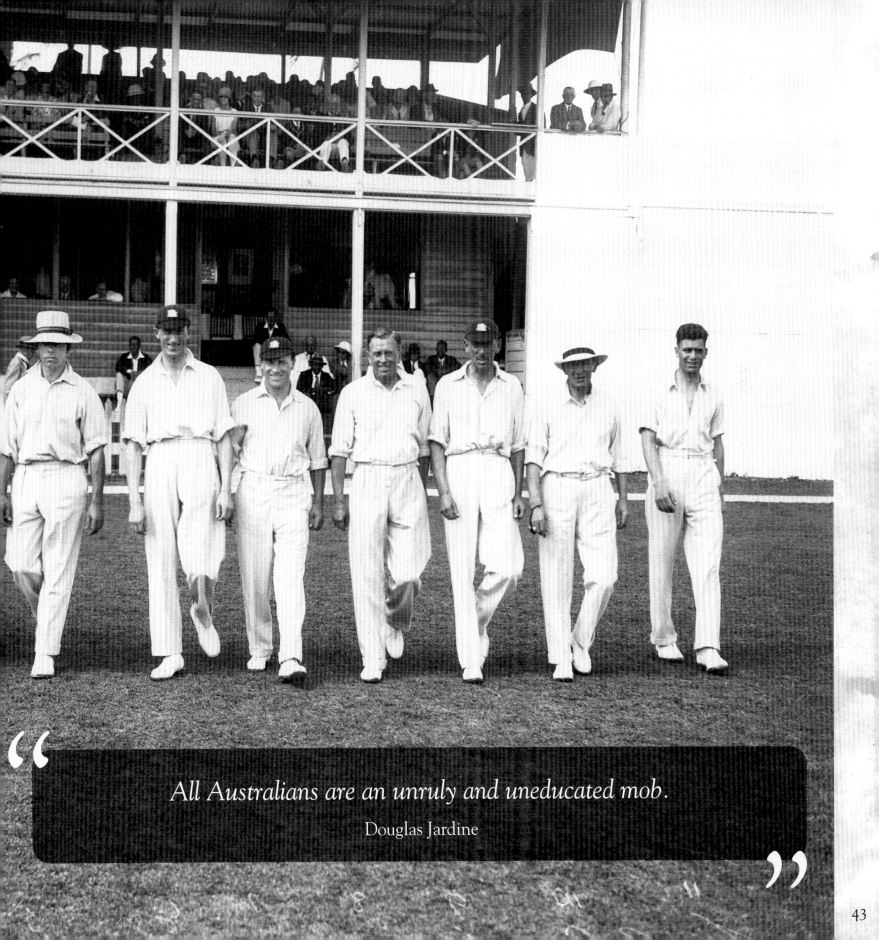

> *All Australians are an unruly and uneducated mob.*
>
> Douglas Jardine

As a mode of play, Bodyline was highly effective. England won the first Test in Sydney, and while the Aussies recovered to take the second Test in Melbourne, England dominated the rest of the series.

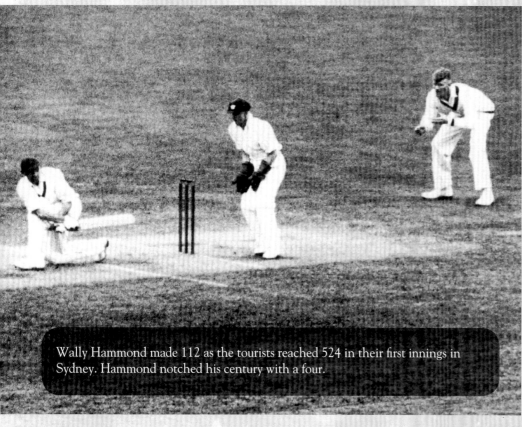

Wally Hammond made 112 as the tourists reached 524 in their first innings in Sydney. Hammond notched his century with a four.

The wondrously named Nawab of Pataudi contributed 102 runs to England's huge first innings total.

Hammond smashes O'Reilly for six in Sydney.

ABOVE: On the second day of the first Test, Bob Wyatt survived a run-out when he made ground before Jack Singleton could hit his wicket.

The rancour caused by "fast leg theory" contributed to a series marked for the level of sledging. On-field mockery and abuse was nothing new in the game, and neither was the barracking from the home crowd, but the 1932–33 series saw the vocal exchanges taken to new levels, with the parentage of several English players called into question by spectators.

RIGHT: Australia's Bert Oldfield reached for home on day two. After a home win in Melbourne, it was the third Test at Adelaide when matters turned really nasty, and Oldfield was one of those on the receiving end. A ferocious spell of fast bowling from Larwood accounted for two worrying injuries: first skipper Bill Woodfull and then Oldfield succumbed; the latter collapsing after being struck on the head. Larwood was not actually bowling Bodyline-style for these particular deliveries, but it added to the poisonous atmosphere. *Wisden*'s view was that it was "probably the most unpleasant Test ever played".

ABOVE: The aggressive bowling wasn't all one way: Gubby Allen was hurt by a delivery from Australia's Lisle Nagel.

Whatever the rights and wrongs of England's bowling methods, it reaped dividends. Bradman's average was cut down from the high 90s to 56.57, and his compatriots could do little to stem the flow of wickets. The anger in the stands and away from the Test venues intensified. There were fears of riots among the home crowd, and Harold Larwood was the focus of much of the home ire.

After Adelaide, the Australian Board of Control for Cricket sent a telegram to the MCC in which Bodyline was described as a menace to the game. More controversial was the use of the term "unsporting" – a direct challenge to the body that had long prided and congratulated itself on its probity and fair-minded values. The ABCC demanded the tactic cease, making inevitable headlines and leading to comments from outraged politicians and the very real threat of a diplomatic row.

Jardine feared he would be hung out to dry for the furore by the MCC; instead, the ABCC withdrew the accusation of unsportsmanlike behaviour. But once the series was over, the cricket establishment found a scapegoat. It was not Jardine but Larwood – and Voce – who were requested to publically apologize by way of a signed letter. Larwood refused – and never played for England again. It laid bare the suffocating hypocrisy of the class distinctions that plagued the English game: Gubby Allen (educated at Eton and Cambridge) had refused to bowl Bodyline despite Jardine's insistence; Larwood, the miner from the Nottinghamshire coalfields, simply followed orders – and paid the price.

ABOVE: Larwood at home with Nottinghamshire in May 1928.

RIGHT: Larwood was one of the world's fastest bowlers but no mean batsman either, with a first-class high score of 102.

> *Larwood is not to be compared to the greats of the past but he has his moments.*
>
> *The Times, 1932*

LEFT: Larwood was the stereotypical fast-bowling son of the soil. He hailed from a Nottinghamshire mining community of Nuncargate and went down the pit himself before cricket provided a professional escape. In 1949 he emigrated to Australia, where he received an altogether warmer welcome than during that notorious southern-hemisphere summer of 1932–33.

ABOVE: The controversy made front-page news. On 24th January 1933 the *Daily Mirror* reported the MCC's stinging response to the Australian cable.

A smiling Jardine returns home to Greenock in May 1933, disembarking from the tender the *Duchess of Fife* after leaving the ship *Duchess of Atholl* that had brought the team back from their tour. The captain sat out the next Ashes series and never played against Australia again, his absence helping to turn down the temperature of what had become a heated rivalry.

On the pitch, Jardine was calculating, cold and uncompromising to the point of obsession. Off it, he was said to be witty, sociable and loyal to friends. To the end he was unapologetic about Bodyline: Jardine was an England captain who played to win.

> " *A great fighter, a grand friend and an unforgiving enemy.*
>
> Bill Bowes on his captain, Douglas Jardine "

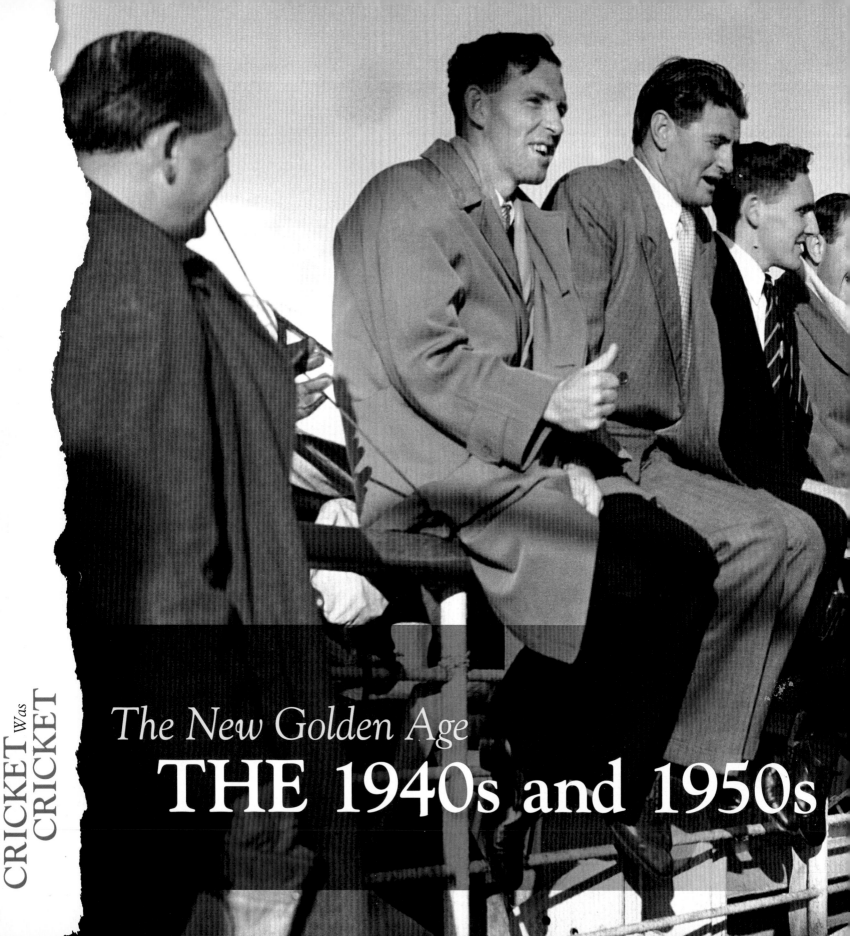

The New Golden Age
THE 1940s and 1950s

All aboard for England. The 1953 Australian tour party arrive suitably attired for the cooler climes of northern Europe in April. The summer may have been a damp squib weather-wise, but it was a landmark series and a momentous era as a whole for the Ashes.

With war finally over, but years of austerity to come, sport provided a sense of restoration and a welcome relief from the often bitter realities of a long, hard recovery from six years of conflict. The timeless appeal of cricket occupied a vital role in this regard, and the Ashes in particular seemed to embody a return to normality.

It was certainly business as usual in the first years of resumed Ashes contests, as Australia continued to dominate. Wally Hammond may have called it a day at the end of the 1946–47 series, but Don Bradman continued to perform at the highest level, playing a fundamental part in his side's 3-0 win.

The Don finally hung up his Ashes bat in 1948, signing off with yet another prodigious haul of runs as his side enjoyed a 4-0 rout, leading to the team of many talents being dubbed the "Invincibles". Their infallibility was never better illustrated than at Headingley, when the Aussies scored a record 404 on the final day to win, with Bradman scoring 173 and Arthur Morris 182. The only fly in the Australian ointment was Bradman's duck in the final Test at The Oval, which prevented him registering a Test average of 100 or more: 99.94 was Bradman's phenomenal mark instead.

If England thought Bradman's absence in 1950–51 would ring the changes they were to be rudely disappointed. The visitors lacked strength in depth and experience and were soundly beaten 4-1. They did at least win a match – their first Ashes success for almost 13 years, and it hinted at change to come.

By 1953, England were at last in a position to compete, with a number of top players to call on, including Len Hutton (England's first professional captain), Alec Bedser, Denis Compton and Trevor Bailey. A weather-curtailed series ended with a dramatic win at The Oval, to earn England the Ashes for the first time in 19 years; the game was enjoyed in more homes than ever before via the medium of television. The English feel-good factor continued with victories in 1954–55 in which Frank "Typhoon" Tyson caused a pace-bowling storm, and 1956, the latter featuring Jim Laker's record 19-wicket haul, with murmurings about customized pitches – a feature of the decade. But the Aussies struck back with a convincing, if hardly scintillating, 4-0 win in 1958–59. England complained about the actions of some of the bowlers, but Richie Benaud's side were the coming force in Ashes cricket.

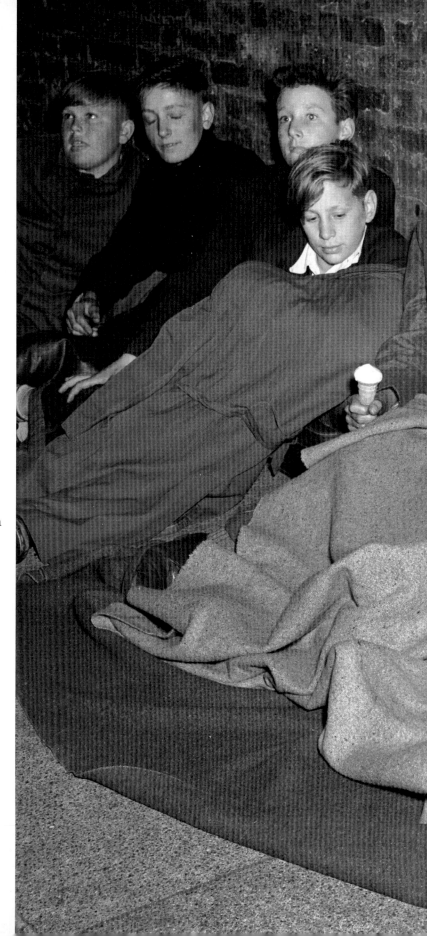

Settling down for the night with an ice cream, a group of excited boys made sure they were at the front of the queue for entry to the climactic last day of the fifth Text at The Oval in August 1953. The series denouement captivated the nation like few other sporting events.

Invincibles

LEFT: Keith Miller pulls one deep in 1948 but was caught on the boundary. A key figure in the "Invincibles" Australian side of the era, Miller was an avuncular character who lived life to the full. His experiences as a wartime RAAF fighter pilot gave him a distinct perspective on the importance of the game. A genuine all-rounder, he formed a lethally effective bowling partnership with Ray Lindwall, while his accomplished batting was as entertaining as it was effective.

> *Pressure is a Messerschmitt up your arse; playing cricket is not.*
>
> Keith Miller

RIGHT: Denis Compton grabbed a single in the third Test in July 1948 to keep the bowling of Bill Johnston away from Godfrey Evans and maintain strike. Compton scored a superb and brave unbeaten 145, the achievement receiving added plaudits in consideration of the fact that Compton had been hit by a ball early in his innings, receiving a cut that required stitches, and forced a temporary rest. For all Compton's heroics, poor weather intervened, and England had to settle for a draw even though defeat of the superb Australian side was a distinct possibility.

Production values: the Australian touring party of 1953 were honoured guests at a surprise tour of a Heinz factory at Harlesden, West London.

Lindsay Hassett's team were missing a key figure in the retired Bradman, but, amid a series played with great spirit and sportsmanship, they were popular visitors around the country, and made quite an impression at the Heinz plant. There were handshakes and tomato ketchup bottles all round in the canteen, where Heinz's Sir Frank Shires presented a special baby tumbler to the Aussie's Alan Davidson (below) for his baby son, who had been born while his father was on tour.

The players did their best to maintain their interest and hide their disappointment at losing the series, while female employees packed a famous 57 varieties of sauces, canned goods and assorted foodstuffs (opposite right). By remarkable coincidence England had won their 57th Test match against Australia the day before at The Oval to win the Ashes.

LEFT: The visiting players, including Ron Archer, signed a special cricket bat, which would later take pride of place in Heinz's "57 Club" trophy cabinet.

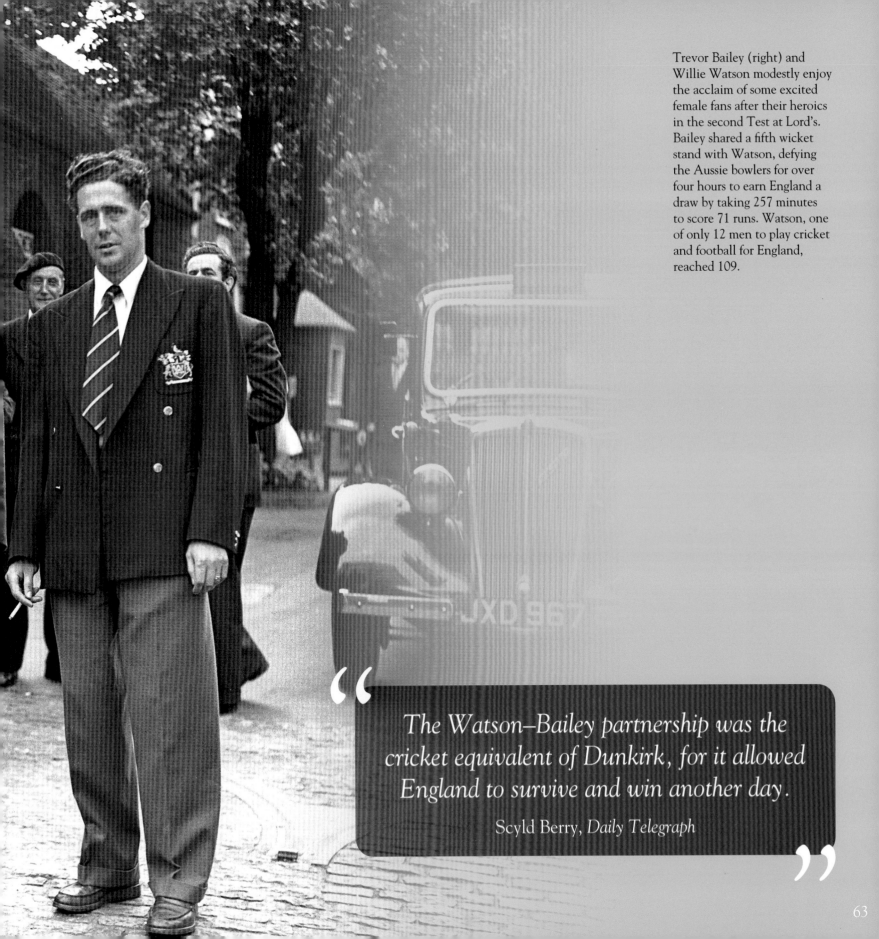

Trevor Bailey (right) and Willie Watson modestly enjoy the acclaim of some excited female fans after their heroics in the second Test at Lord's. Bailey shared a fifth wicket stand with Watson, defying the Aussie bowlers for over four hours to earn England a draw by taking 257 minutes to score 71 runs. Watson, one of only 12 men to play cricket and football for England, reached 109.

> " The Watson–Bailey partnership was the cricket equivalent of Dunkirk, for it allowed England to survive and win another day. "
>
> Scyld Berry, *Daily Telegraph*

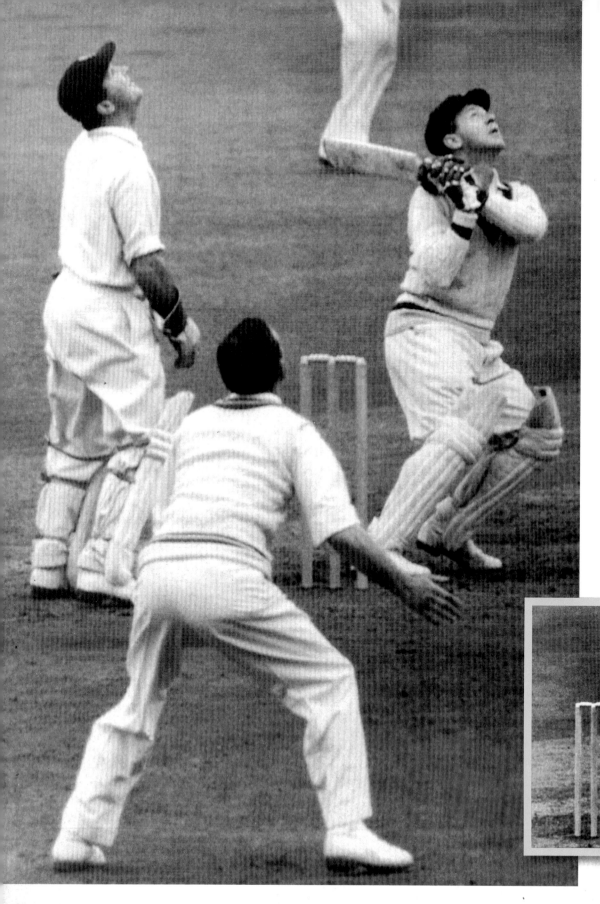

LEFT: The 1953 Ashes was a fascinating series of ebb and flow. The first four matches may have ended as draws, but there was a mounting sense of tension and excitement, with both sides threatening to take advantage before either being hauled back by the opposition or the weather intervening.

In the first Test at Trent Bridge, the visitors' Arthur Morris skied a delivery from Roy Tattersall, but it was Alec Bedser who did most of the bowling damage for England. He took 39 wickets in the 1953 series.

BELOW: Keith Miller ducked a ball from Trevor Bailey on the second day at Nottingham.

BELOW: Keith Miller (left) and Lindsay Hassett limbered up for the third Test at Old Trafford – another draw plagued by rain, though the Aussies lost eight wickets for just 35 runs in their second innings.

RIGHT: By July and the Headingley Test, the two teams could still not be separated. The day before the match started, there was concern in the England camp, with Tony Lock showing his injured finger to squad member Brian Statham. In the face of fierce bowling from Lindwall and co., England were on the defensive for much of the match but held on for the draw.

Fans Frenzy

The 1950s was an era marked for its pride in a stiff upper lip, with none of the emotional fripperies associated with excitable foreigners – but only in some traditionalist English quarters. The 1953 Ashes thrilled the public like few other sporting contests had for a generation, and the crowd scenes from the time illustrate just how much.

ABOVE: Fans throng the streets around Headingley before the first day of the fourth Test in Leeds.

ABOVE: Carry on cricket camping: fans bed down for the night on the eve of the third day of the climactic Test at The Oval.

RIGHT: Young fans went to all sorts of lengths (and heights) to gain a view as England homed in on a sensational victory at The Oval.

The early 1950s was a time when great changes were starting to take place in Britain. While rationing would not end until 1954, national service was still in force and much of the country still bore the battered legacy of the war, the austerity years were drawing to a close, and there were new and exciting products for members of the "consumer society" to buy – television foremost among them.

By 1953, 21 per cent of households had a set, and great events became "TV events". The Coronation of 1953 was one such spectacle, and the fifth Test of the Ashes series was another. On the third day of the match, a crowd gathered in The Falcon pub in London's Fetter Lane to watch the nail-biting action from the comfort of the bar – albeit on a tiny monochrome screen.

It's the Ashes! At 2.57pm Denis Compton drives a four off Morris, hitting the winning run on the final day at The Oval and, with it, England win the Ashes for the first time since 1934.

The Cricket Icon

Denis Compton emerged as a teenage prodigy spotted by, among others, the great Sir Pelham Warner. The young Compton soon realized his potential and went on to flourish as one of England's greatest sporting icons. Other players may have registered better Ashes records, but few could match Compton for personality and impact. He was the darling of English cricket either side of the war, embodied this new golden age for the sport among England supporters and, with his adverts for Brylcreem, represented the sporting star as a celebrity personality with commercial appeal.

Compton scored a century in his first meeting with Australia in 1938 – one of five Ashes tons – and a match-saving unbeaten 76 at Lord's later in the series. The former Lord's staffer saw his career interrupted by wartime service, but in 1948 he provided the ray of hope for England in an otherwise dispiriting series. By the time 1953 came round, he was into his thirties and debilitated by a long-standing knee problem, but could still produce world-class performances, and it was fitting that this heroic figure should hit the winning runs.

With his carefree style, daring, charisma and good looks, which endeared him to an audience well beyond the boundary rope, Compton was a man reared in the traditionalist past but firmly suiting the role of a modern hero. He was also a successful footballer, playing for Arsenal and in wartime matches for England alongside his brother Leslie.

MAN OF THE
– ERA –

Denis Compton

Compton passes on some tips to 5-year-old Robin Lawrie in the sports shop owned by Arsenal team-mate Wally Barnes in Haringey, north London.

ASHES
— SCORECARD —

Denis Compton

Name: Denis Compton

Born: 1918

Appearances: 28

High score: 184 (Trent Bridge, 1948)

Batting average: 42.84

Best figures: 1-21 (Lord's, 1953)

Bowling average: 99.33

ABOVE: The Compton brothers, Denis (centre) and Leslie, besieged by autograph hunters at Lord's, with the former casting a none-too-friendly glare towards the cameraman.

73

LEFT & BELOW: Ecstatic crowds spilled onto The Oval pitch to celebrate the 1953 series win.

ABOVE: At the home of skipper Len Hutton in Pudsey, Yorkshire, the Union Jack was flown high in August 1953. Hutton – England's first professional skipper – was the resolute and inspirational leader of the victorious England side – he was a wonderful batsman and a true gentleman, who was knighted in 1956.

Those boys who scaled The Oval wall to catch a glimpse of their heroes in action (see page 67) were well placed to view the celebrations.

After Hutton led England to another series win in 1954–55, he relinquished the captaincy to Peter May, but was on hand to greet Aussie skipper Ian Johnson on the arrival of the tourists in April 1956. Newsreel cameras also captured the moment for posterity.

While his side could not regain the Ashes in the face of England's highly effective mix of pace and spin, Colin McDonald was the pick of the visiting batsmen.

Richie Benaud and Neil Harvey share a moment at the nets at Old Trafford during training, before the fourth Test in 1956.

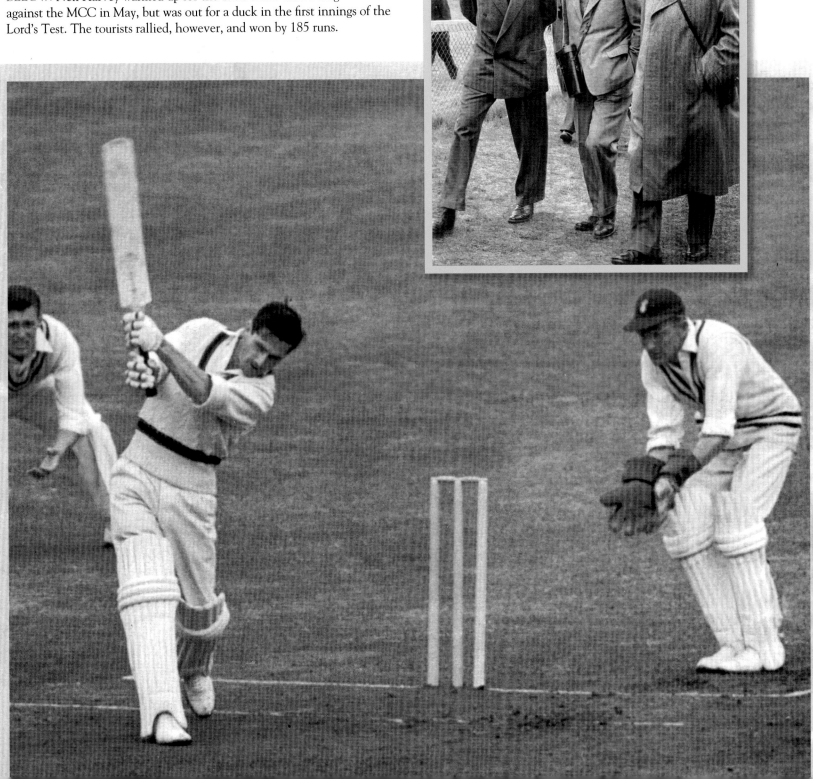

RIGHT: Keith Miller (left) was a keen racegoer and made the most of the Australian team's visit to Epsom races in April 1956, sharing tips and laughs with the Duke of Norfolk and Lord Rosebery.

BELOW: Neil Harvey warmed up for the 1956 series with a magnificent 225 against the MCC in May, but was out for a duck in the first innings of the Lord's Test. The tourists rallied, however, and won by 185 runs.

ABOVE: Cyril Washbrook on his way to 98 in the third Test at Headingley. Along with Peter May's 101, the knock did much to ensure England's emphatic victory, which drew the sides level, and Washbrook received suitable acclaim from the Leeds crowd (right).

Australian hopes following the Lord's Test were swiftly dashed when England won by an innings and 42 runs at Headingley, with Jim Laker's 11-wicket haul a major contributory factor. Laker was merely warming up, however: his world-record 19 wickets for just 90 runs in the Old Trafford meeting (leading to a win by an innings and 170 runs) was one of the finest achievements in all of sport during the 1950s – or any other decade, for that matter.

Laker was pictured with his wife Lilly leaving their hotel after Jim's astonishing feat of spin bowling. The pair had met in Egypt when he was serving as a British Army sergeant in Egypt during the Second World War.

> "Forget the scorebook, Tony, you played your part, too.
>
> England captain Peter May to Tony Lock, who took the other wicket in the Old Trafford Test of 1956"

ABOVE: Following his extraordinary exploits, Laker was, unsurprisingly, every cricket autograph hunters' prized target.

RIGHT: The big Yorkshireman celebrated modestly with a non-alcoholic pint. His achievement was not without controversy. The Australians seethed, believing that the preparation of the wicket to suit Laker's spin bordered on cheating. "This pitch is an absolute disgrace. What lies in store for Test cricket if the groundsmen are allowed to play the fool like this again?" wrote former spinner Bill O'Reilly. Groundsman Bert Flack responded: "Thank God (president) Nasser has taken over the Suez Canal, otherwise I'd be plastered over every front page like Marilyn Monroe."

RIGHT INSET: Great Laker: the scoreboard told the incredible tale.

Fifth day's play
TEST AT A GLANCE

ENGLAND.—First Innings: 459 (Sheppard 113, Richardson 104, Cowdrey 80; Johnson 4 for 151). Balls received 951, fours 55.

AUSTRALIA.—First Innings: 84 (Laker 9 for 37). Balls received 264, fours 10.

Second Innings
Overnight: 84 for 2).

	Runs	Mins.	Balls Rec'd	Fours
McDonald, c Oakman, b Laker	89	337	316	10
(Volley to short square leg)				
Burke, c Lock, b Laker	33	105	99	4
(Went with break to leg slip)				
Harvey, c Cowdrey, b Laker	0	1	1	0
(Full toss to mid-wicket)				
Craig, lbw, b Laker	38	259	269	5
(Played back, should have been forward)				
Mackay, c Oakman, b Laker	0	8	7	0
(Dabbed feebly into second slip's lap)				
Miller, b Laker	0	15	18	0
(Made into yorker)				
Archer, c Oakman, b Laker	0	2	2	0
(Low to short square leg)				
Benaud, b Laker	18	105	121	3
(Back instead of forward)				
Lindwall, c Lock, b Laker	8	41	34	1
(Straight to backward short leg)				
Johnson, not out	1	25	29	0
Maddocks, lbw, b Laker	2	6	6	0
(Went with arm)				
Extras (b 12, lb 4)	16			
Totals (complete innings)	205	—	902	23

FALL OF WICKETS (contd.): 3-114, 4-124, 5-130, 6-130, 7-181, 8-198, 9-203.

BOWLING: Statham 16-9-15-0; Bailey 20-8-31-0; Laker 51.2-23-53-10; Lock 55-30-69-0; Oakman 8-3-21-0. ENGLAND WON BY AN INNINGS AND 170 RUNS.

England set off for Australia in 1958–59 in confident mood. Buoyed by three successive Ashes series wins, they had restored the fortunes of the game at home and made England a force to be reckoned with once again. But the determined demeanour of skipper Peter May (left) and vice-captain Colin Cowdrey (below) on-board the *Iberia* was ultimately to no avail, as they lost 4-0 to an Australian side reborn under Richie Benaud.

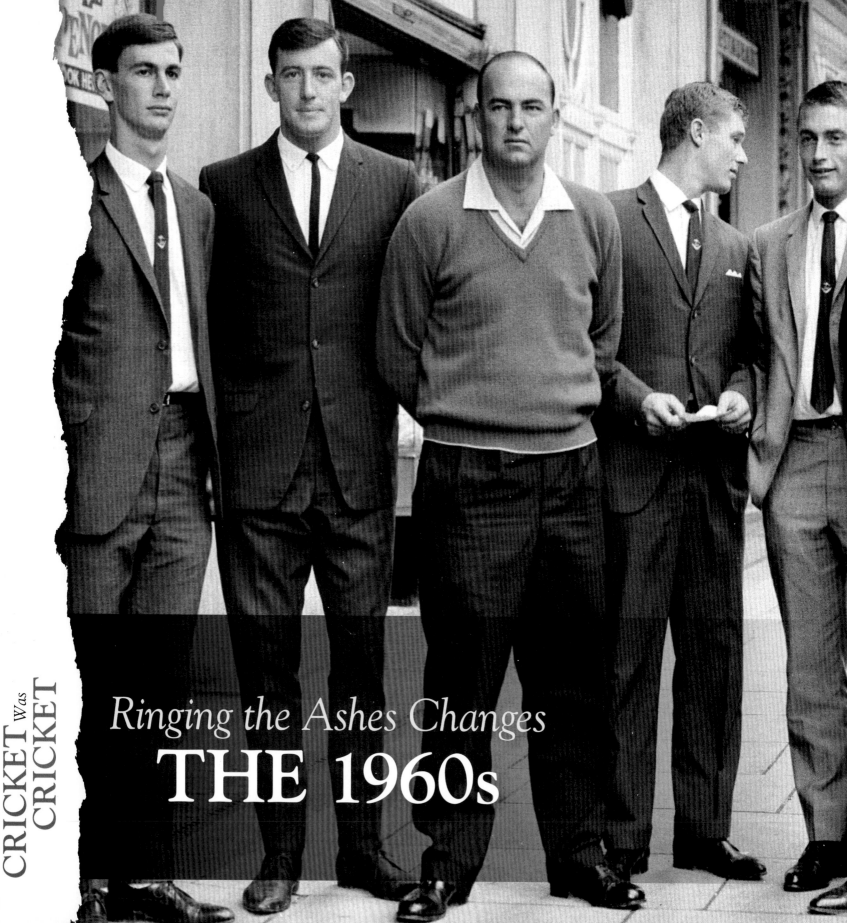

Ringing the Ashes Changes
THE 1960s

The Aussies in besuited style outside the Waldorf Hotel, the team's London base in the spring of 1964.

After the highs of the 1950s, the following decade suffered by comparison. A succession of relatively lacklustre Ashes series was played out to a backdrop of concerns that the Test format was on the wane. Any lack of enthusiasm on the part of the English may have been influenced by another period of Aussie domination.

Travelling to England by sea for the last time, the Australians were once again expertly led by Richie Benaud as they retained the urn in 1961 with a more expansive style than they had displayed in 1958–59. Benaud's spell of five wickets for 12 in just 25 balls at Old Trafford in July 1961 earned an astonishing victory for the visitors.

England travelled to Australia with high hopes in 1962, and victory at Sydney made a series win a distinct possibility, but the home side rallied, and by the end of the series in 1963 had done enough to earn a 1-1 draw and retain the urn.

Bad weather and ponderous play plagued the 1964 series, though Fred Trueman made his mark on cricket history at The Oval by becoming the first bowler to take 300 Test wickets. By the time of the 1965–66 encounter, the convention that the holders would retain the Ashes if a series was drawn was contributing to disquiet over the contest's future. England captain Mike Smith even went so far as to call for the Ashes to be discontinued. The advent of one-day cricket in 1963 and the end of the distinction between "amateurs" and "gentlemen" the year before showed how the once seemingly impregnable traditions of the game were being eroded. Could the age-old rivalry go the same way?

The Ashes survived, but another drawn series in 1968 did little to restore confidence in its future. The furore over the Basil D'Oliveira affair, when the MCC first excluded him from their touring party to South Africa in 1968–69 and then called him up, only for the tour to be cancelled due to the host's policy of apartheid, was one of English cricket's most shameful lows and threw international cricket into turmoil. Now, by way of contrast, the dependable character of the Ashes arguably had more appeal.

The 1961 series was a rather forlorn one for England. The sight of umpires Syd Buller (left) and Frank Lee under umbrellas during the Edgbaston Test, before they ended play on 12th June, seemed to sum up a gloomy home mood.

Welcome to Edgbaston

The 1961 series saw the first Ashes Test staged in the second city since 1909, and both the ground and the people of Birmingham were welcoming hosts.

LEFT: Ground staff choose the stumps for the match.

ABOVE RIGHT: In the ticket office (left to right) Ann Kerr, Mary Williams, Tony Haycock, Mrs Norah Deakins and Pat Craig were hard at work.

RIGHT: Two Birmingham schoolboy cricketers met Richie Benaud, who was holding a bat that featured the signatures of the Aussie captain and his team. It was one of the prizes in an Australian trade fortnight competition in the city.

ABOVE: Benaud got in some net practice …

BELOW: … and had a chat with his England counterpart Colin Cowdrey…

ABOVE: … as Aussie colleague Norm O'Neill (right) and England's Brian Statham (centre) chatted with the Australian team treasurer Mr Steele …

BELOW: … before the visiting side met the press.

The punters turned out in force for a match full of entertainment, with Australia making their highest total in England since 1934 (516-9 declared), and England fighting back with second innings centuries from Raman Subba Row (112) and Ted Dexter (180) that forced a draw.

ABOVE: The Gower Street Secondary Modern School cricket team arrived for the first day.

BELOW: Schoolboys from Wyndcliffe Junior School watched their heroes in action.

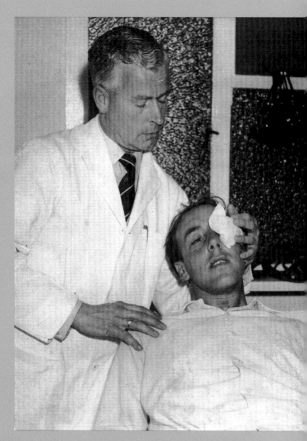

LEFT: England wicket-keeper John Murray took one in the face from a ball delivered by Ray Illingworth. Murray received treatment (right) for a resulting cut. Murray at one stage held the world record of 1,527 wicket-keeping dismissals.

BELOW: Mr James Laurie from Niagara Falls, Canada, made sure he was in attendance at Edgbaston. The 69-year-old had travelled to England for every Ashes Test series since the war.

Sadly for Edgbaston, rain marred the match and effectively put paid to a positive result. The Australians dashed for cover on the first day, and the spectators followed suit or attempted to put a brave face on a typical English summer two days later (above and below). Nonetheless, the match had been a success in terms of its popularity, with a record crowd of 25,000 on the third day.

LEFT: Colin Cowdrey thanked the Edgbaston ground staff team for their efforts to ensure as much play as possible.

BELOW: Umpires Syd Buller and Frank Lee inspecting the wicket with groundsman Bernard Flack on 12th June 1961, before play was abandoned for the day due to rain.

Fred Trueman's high level of performance in the early 1960s was an admonishment to the selectors who had left him out of the England side in the 1950s. In a period when English batsmen struggled and results against the Aussies were generally poor, the efforts of the bowlers were some compensation and "Fiery Fred" provided some much needed pride.

England badly needed Trueman's natural competitiveness. A tough, often gruff, and occasionally rough Yorkshireman, he challenged authority and paid the price with various charges that enforced his absence from a number of line-ups. Trueman's speed and style turned him into one of the world's top bowlers and, in tandem with Brian Statham, one half of a lethally effective fast-bowling partnership.

Trueman's finest Ashes hour came in the third Test of 1961 at Leeds. With two devastatingly effective spells, he engineered England's solitary triumph in the series. On the first day he ripped through the Australian order to take five wickets for just 16 runs. He followed that up with an even more scintillating performance on the Saturday, taking another five wickets, with just 24 deliveries, without conceding a single run. In the end he returned figures of 6 for 30 with a cumulative match total of 11 wickets for 88.

Trueman ended his meetings with Australia in 1964, 11 years after the Aussie batsmen had first encountered his pace and power. It is safe to assume they were glad to see the back of him.

MAN OF THE
– ERA –
Fred Trueman

Fiery Fred limbering up for action.

> *Use every weapon within the rules and stretch the rules to breaking point, I say.*
>
> Fred Trueman

ASHES
— SCORECARD —
Fred Trueman

Name: Fred Trueman

Born: 1931

Appearances: 19

High score: 38 (Adelaide, 1963)

Batting average: 12.07

Best figures: 6-30 (Headingley, 1961)

Bowling average: 25.30

BELOW: Trueman acknowledges the acclaim of the crowd after his 5 for 58 on 6th July 1961.

LEFT: Trueman was a celebrity in his playing days and stayed in the limelight in Test cricket retirement, rubbing shoulders with footballer Bobby Charlton at a 1968 Variety Club of Great Britain luncheon at the Savoy Hotel.

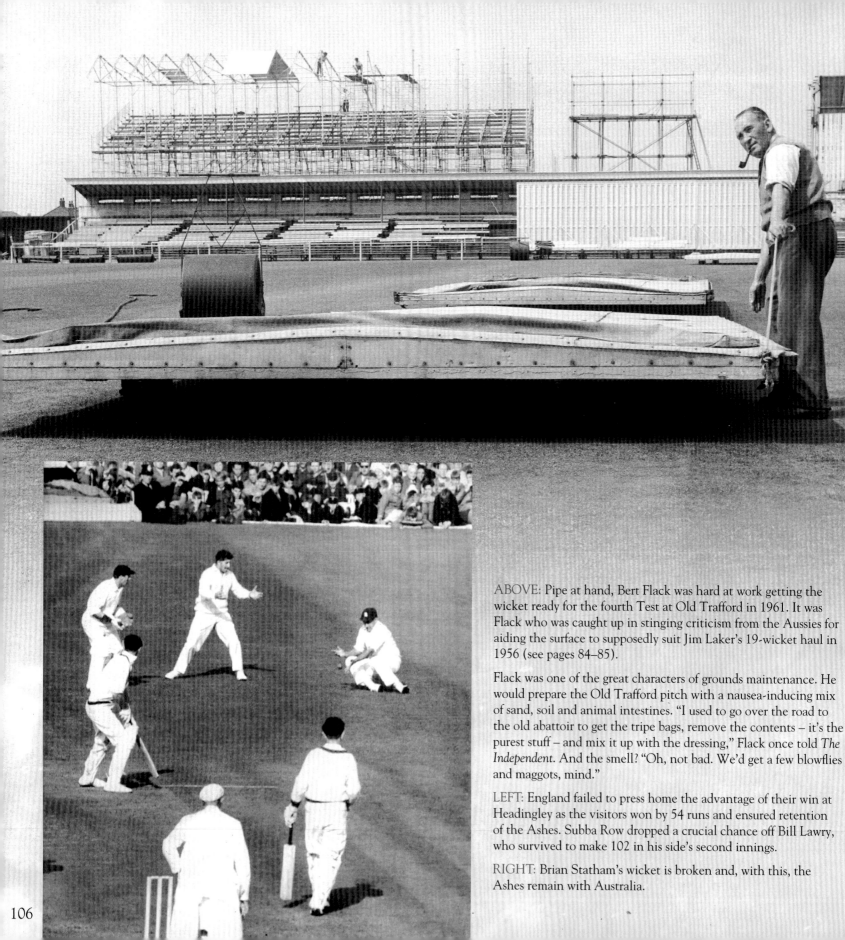

ABOVE: Pipe at hand, Bert Flack was hard at work getting the wicket ready for the fourth Test at Old Trafford in 1961. It was Flack who was caught up in stinging criticism from the Aussies for aiding the surface to supposedly suit Jim Laker's 19-wicket haul in 1956 (see pages 84–85).

Flack was one of the great characters of grounds maintenance. He would prepare the Old Trafford pitch with a nausea-inducing mix of sand, soil and animal intestines. "I used to go over the road to the old abattoir to get the tripe bags, remove the contents – it's the purest stuff – and mix it up with the dressing," Flack once told *The Independent*. And the smell? "Oh, not bad. We'd get a few blowflies and maggots, mind."

LEFT: England failed to press home the advantage of their win at Headingley as the visitors won by 54 runs and ensured retention of the Ashes. Subba Row dropped a crucial chance off Bill Lawry, who survived to make 102 in his side's second innings.

RIGHT: Brian Statham's wicket is broken and, with this, the Ashes remain with Australia.

Fred Trueman enjoyed an Ashes swansong in the Melbourne Test in 1962–63 but another drawn series meant that by the time the Australians returned to the UK in 1964, the Ashes urn was still in their hands – and remained so after another rain-hit summer. The visitors' Graham McKenzie (left) and Grahame Corling took shelter from the downpour at Old Trafford before the fourth Test. The game itself ended in a draw after the two teams made a combined first innings total of 1,267 runs.

ABOVE: In a tour match at Worcester in April 1964, Norman O'Neill (third from left) received a telegram telling him that his wife had given birth to a son. He was congratulated by colleagues (left to right) Barry Jarman, Bobby Simpson and Corling.

LEFT: With the retirements of Benaud, Neil Harvey and Alan Davidson, the Australians were supposedly weakened but they managed to keep England at bay and won the series 1-0. Simpson had taken over the captaincy and, with the series decided, enjoyed a friendly round of golf with Brian Close and Denis Compton.

ABOVE: Here comes the rain again … Groundsman Ian Guys tried to clear water from the pitch at Edgbaston ahead of the third Test in 1968.

England had taken a promising lead in the 1965–66 series thanks to victory by an innings at Sydney, but, lacking a decisive cutting edge in their bowling, the series ended in another draw. English frustrations continued two years later, and not solely due to the weather. Poor fielding cost them the opener at Old Trafford, poor conditions entailed a draw at Lord's, and after a positive start in Birmingham the hosts could not produce the victory that might have enabled them to win back the Ashes.

RIGHT: Colin Cowdrey won the toss against Bill Lawry at Edgbaston. The pair were injured for the next match at Leeds and had to be replaced by Tom Graveney and Barry Jarman.

ABOVE: England claimed the wicket of Alan Connolly in the first innings, with wicket-keeper Alan Knott and slip fielder Ken Barrington celebrating bowler Ray Illingworth's successful delivery.

ABOVE: How's that?
Australian players gather
around John Edrich after
he had been rapped on
the hand by a ball from
Eric Freeman.

RIGHT: Another chance
goes begging as Colin
Cowdrey misses the
opportunity to dismiss
Ian Chappell.

Ashes
ARENAS

The world's greatest cricket rivalry has been played out at the finest stadiums on opposite ends of the earth, and, in England, the best grounds have long vied for the prestige of hosting an Ashes Test. Here are portraits through the years of some of the venues.

Lord's

Fitting a new roof at the home of cricket – Lord's – in 1957. The London stadium has never been a particularly accommodating ground for England; the home side has recorded just six victories in 34 matches and have won only twice since 1896 (1934 and 2009).

ABOVE: The view over HQ. Jonathan Cree, son of Dr Cree, looks out through binoculars from the balcony of his father's ninth floor flat in a block called Lord's View in August 1965.

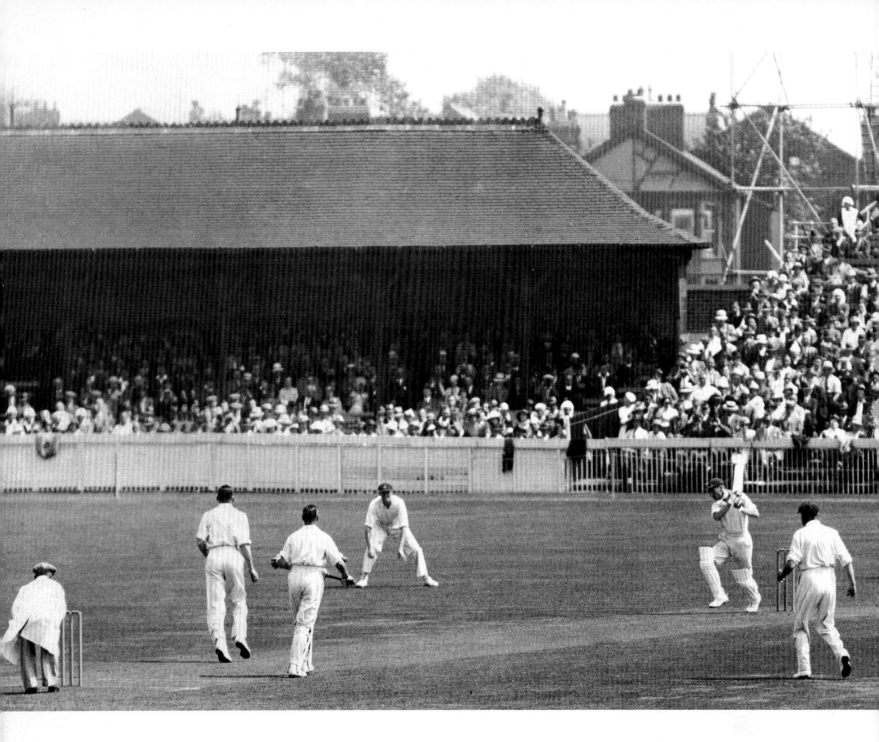

Old Trafford

ABOVE: Mancunian action from the third Test in July 1934. Draws had been the usual order of the day at Old Trafford, with 14 in 28 matches.

RIGHT: Hardy spectators brave leaden Manchester skies in the first Test in 1972.

The Oval

LEFT: No greater number of Ashes matches have been played in England than at The Oval. The home of county side Surrey has long been viewed as a more vibrant alternative to the restrained Lord's and, perhaps for that reason, has produced more fluent England performances. The home side has won 16 times against the Aussies in SE11.

BELOW: In 1947, the gasometer lurked in the background: a world-famous feature that has become a symbol of the stadium.

Edgbaston

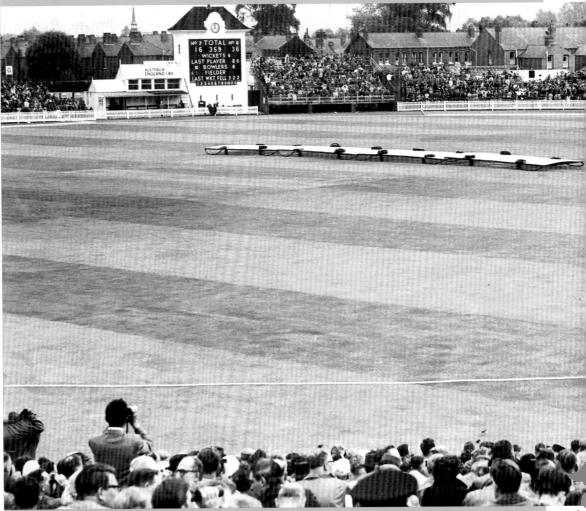

Two views of Edgbaston in Birmingham – in 1961 (above) and 2003 (left). The ground hosted its first Ashes match in 1902.

LEFT: The White Rose county of Yorkshire has long been one of cricket's – and the Ashes' – heartlands. Test matches against Australia have been played in Leeds 24 times, and Headingley played host for the first time in 1899.

The cricket pitch has long co-existed with the rugby ground (as can be seen here in 1933).

Headingley

BELOW: Headingley in 1930. Don Bradman scored his famous 334 here that year.

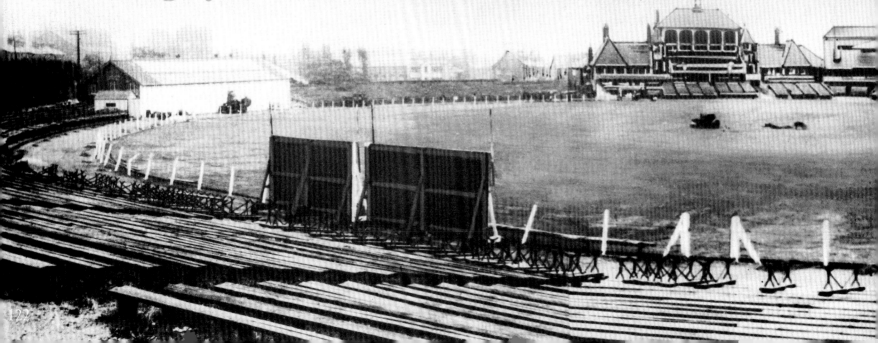

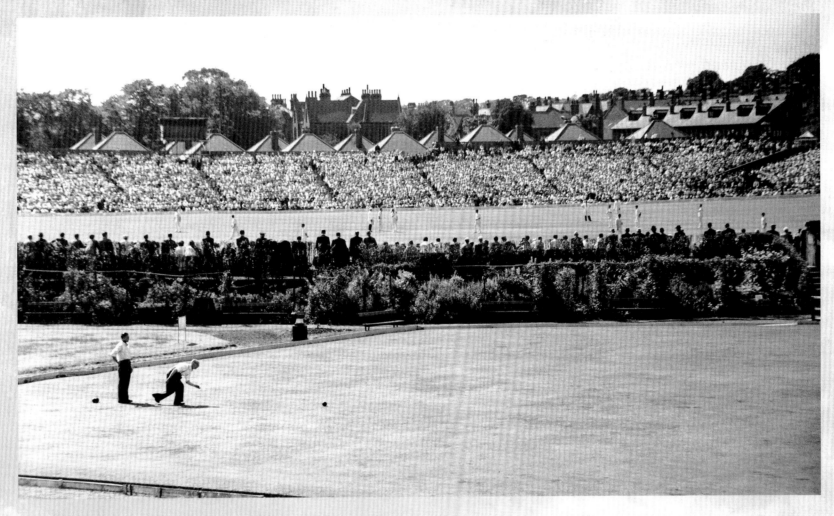

ABOVE: A vital Headingley Test match in 1961? No matter – a gentle game of bowls cannot be interrupted.

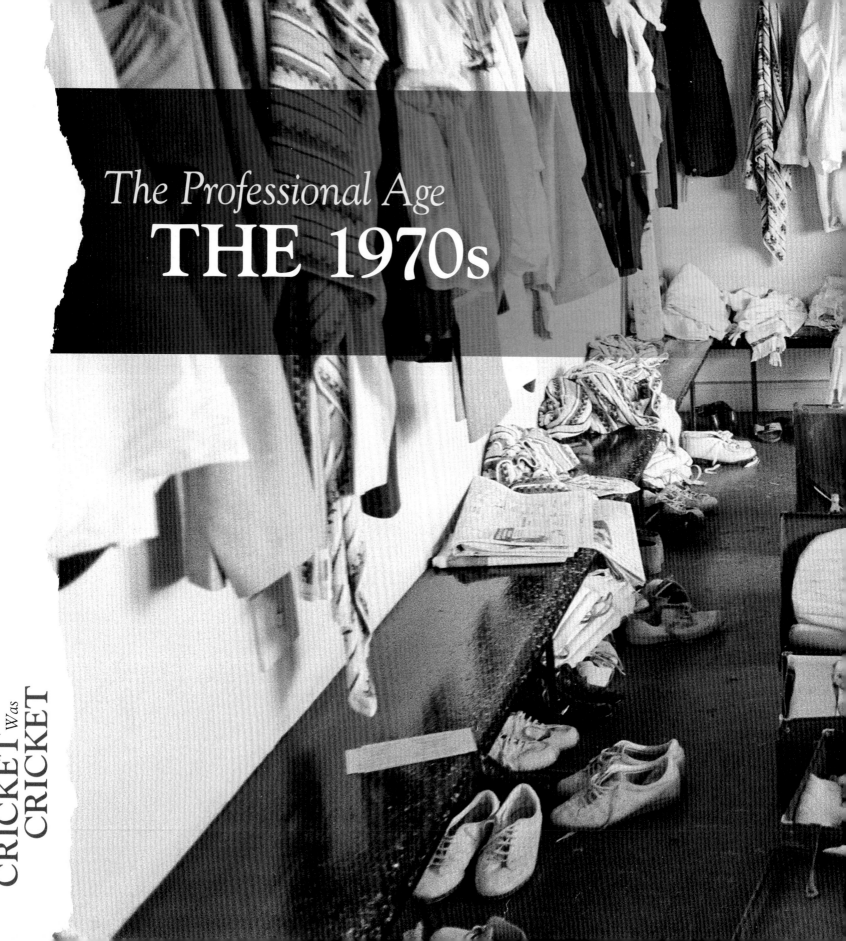

The Professional Age
THE 1970s

.GIFFORD.
ESTERSHIRE C.C.C.

All quiet on the dressing-room front … The scene in the England camp
on day one of the first Test at Old Trafford in 1972.

Modernization – and some pretty fundamental developments at that – were in the Ashes air. While the old adversaries swapped ownership of the urn to make the period one of the more competitive in the contest's history, a more professional approach and off-the-field events helped to make the 1970s one of the more compelling decades.

England began the era with a bang, bringing home the Ashes from the 1970–71 tour, thanks to the efforts of a side that married each aspect of the game more effectively than in previous years. This didn't go down well with the home crowd, and bowler John Snow was subjected to ferocious and occasionally physical barracking at Melbourne. Ray Illingworth's team was already showing signs of age, however, and while the home-soil series was drawn in 1972, momentum was with the visitors. Led by Ian Chappell who imbued a more determined and, as many suggested, more ruthless approach, the Australians were becoming a truly great team. Inspired by the bowling of Dennis Lillee and Jeff Thomson, they walked the 1974–75 series 4-1 and followed that up with a narrow 1-0 series victory in 1975.

The ferocious bowling of the Aussie pair was broadcast in colour (an Ashes first) and reflected the growing influence of television – a factor rendered more notable by the World Series Cricket saga. When his more lucrative TV rights offer was rejected in favour of the Australian state broadcaster's deal, media mogul Kerry Packer set up the rival WSC and tempted the world's best to play in a rival series of "Test" matches for greatly increased pay. The upstart competition threw cricket into disarray.

The Centenary Test was staged in March 1977 – without the Ashes at stake – to commemorate the anniversary of the very first meeting between recognized English and Australian sides in Melbourne in 1877. Remarkably, the outcome was the same: the Aussies won by 45 runs. But amid the WSC furore, a weakened Australian team was twice well beaten by England in 1977 (the first series against the Australians to be sponsored) and 1978–79, as the Ashes contests resumed.

Preparing to give the Aussies a typical English summer welcome, Lord's assistant head groundsman Alec Gull watered the surface of cricket HQ in April 1972.

> *A cricketer of effect rather than the graces.*
>
> John Arlott, on Ian Chappell

The Australians were led in 1972 by Ian Chappell, here presenting the youthful team to the media at the Waldorf. The captain's style dictated how the side would approach the game for a generation or more.

Coming from a family in which a competitive spirit was keenly fostered – his grandfather Vic Richardson and brother Greg also skippered in the baggy green cap, while brother Trevor played for the national side – Ian was a blunt, often bolshie but brilliant leader, with a determined, very professional and very modern view on how the game should be played. Sledging, as a form of gamesmanship, was not new but was believed to have become more prominent under Ian Chappell's reign.

Another tour, another celebration. Jeffrey "Bomber" Hammond reached his 22nd birthday and was toasted by his squad-mates.

The 1972 tour began at a chilly Old Trafford in early June. The mower was out to prepare the wicket (below). Australia celebrated (right) as Johnny Gleeson took the prize wicket of Geoffrey Boycott, trapping the Yorkshireman LBW, but England still won by 89 runs.

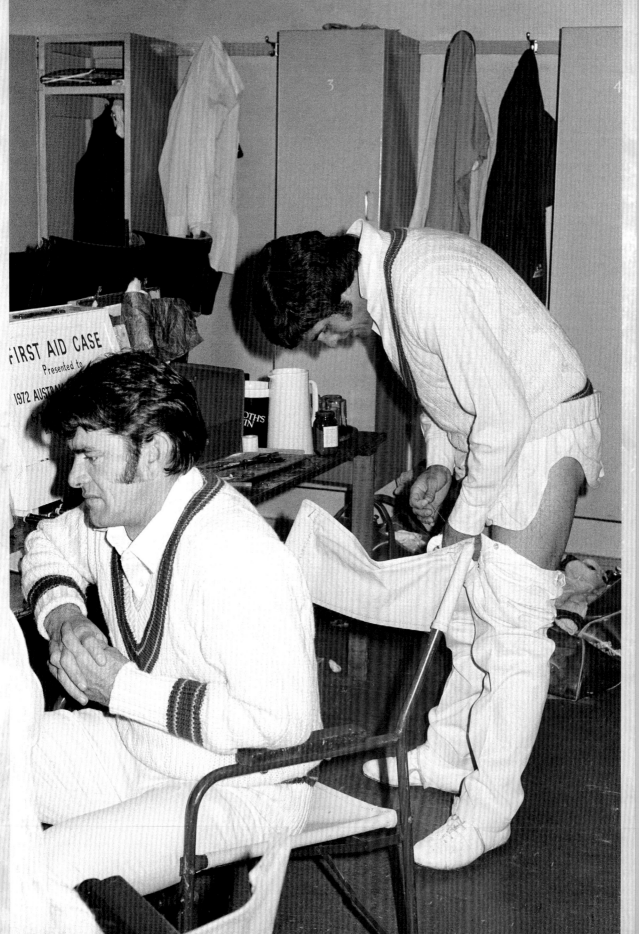

Meanwhile, in the Australian dressing room in Manchester, it was a case of card sharks (right) and (perhaps?) waiting for the new ball (left).

For England's Tony Greig, it was a case of putting his large feet up and relaxing his 6' 6'' frame to mark the victory with a pint (right). Greig, who sadly passed away in 2012, had top-scored in both England innings to play a significant part in his team's win.

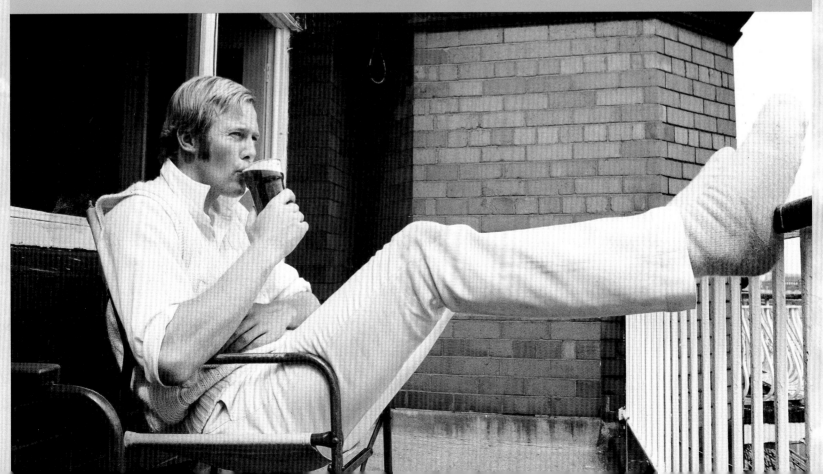

Johnny Gleeson was applauded off the field after his gallant but unsuccessful attempt to help his side bat out the final day. Gleeson was accompanied by a young Dennis Lillee who failed to get off the mark, but it was Lillee's feats with the ball that made his legendary name.

Off to London and England's traditional Test graveyard. The omens were rarely good at Lord's and Australia duly won by the handsome margin of eight wickets. England's star all-rounder of 1909–34, Frank Woolley, was on hand to witness his successors' defeat.

Cricket fan Jilli Wale of Kensington pictured working as a programme seller at Lord's on the first day.

Australia's victory hinged on a fine all-round team effort but two excellent individual displays did make an impact. On his way to an aggressive 131, Greg Chappell made things uncomfortable for the close-fielding Illingworth.

The first day of the 1972 Lord's Test began with supporters taking cover from the drizzle (above), but by day two they were basking in glorious sunshine (below). The same couldn't be said for the England batsmen, faced with the twin-pronged pace attack of Bob Massie and Lillee.

RIGHT: Lillee played his full part in restricting the England batsmen, but it was Bob Massie who really gained victory for the team: the 25-year-old debutante set an Aussie record total of 16 wickets for just 137 runs. Massie's career may have been short-lived – he only played six Tests – but his arrival was certainly dramatic, and he was deservedly clapped off after taking the final English wicket.

Lillee Rascal

Of all the many world-class fast bowlers English batsmen have had to face in nearly 150 years of meetings with Australia, few, if any, have instilled such trepidation and admiration as Dennis Lillee. A fearsome presence with his dark, untamed locks, hurtling in on a long and full-pelt run-up, Lillee combined intimidating speed with precision, craft, persistence and guile. He was one of the greatest bowlers in any arena – and in the Ashes one of Australia's most reliable and lethal weapons.

He made his Ashes debut in the sixth Test at Adelaide in 1971, and was heralded as the replacement for the retired Alan Davidson. The great young hope made an immediate impression with five wickets, and gave further notice of his talent with 10 scalps in the fifth Test of 1972 at The Oval. In all, he claimed 31 victims in the tour, beating the previous Aussie best set by Clarrie Grimmett (1930) and Graham McKenzie (1964). A spell with Haslingden in the Lancashire League had fostered Lillee's development, the testing pitches imbuing him with greater depth to his repertoire than sheer speed.

Australia reaped the dividend for over a decade more. Lillee set new records, took on and beat the world's best batsmen, and overcame injury to reign supreme. He benefitted from expert partners – whether in tandem with the equally intimidating quickie Jeff Thomson or with Australia's pugnacious and prolific wicket-keeper, Rodney Marsh. Lillee tore through a battered England order in the 1974–75 series in Australia and, alongside Thomson, maintained Australian superiority with a match-winning display in the opening Test of the 1975 series. A combination of World Series Cricket and wear and tear muted Lillee's impact in the late 1970s but he was still a potent force into the next decade, recording his best figures against England in 1981.

MAN OF THE
– ERA –
Dennis Lillee

Former England captain Ted Dexter never faced Lillee in competitive anger but experienced the bowler's fearsome action in a specially arranged shoot for the *Daily Mirror*.

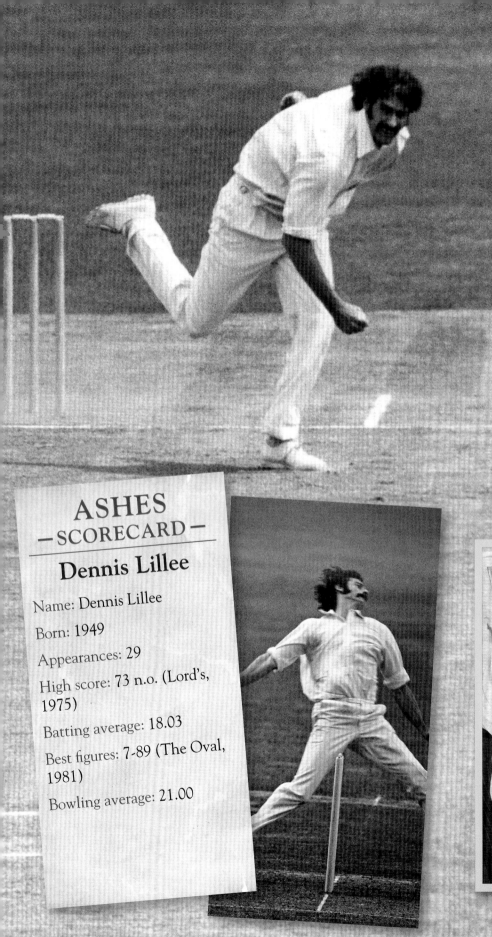

ABOVE: You rang? Lillee was something of a fresh asset in 1972 but England became very familiar with him during the rest of the decade. He was no stranger to controversy, either, and in the 1979–80 series (the Ashes was not contested) he tried – in vain – to use an aluminium bat.

BELOW: Getting the massage treatment on his troublesome back in 1972. Stress fractures had almost ended Lillee's career before it had properly begun, but by (only slightly) diminishing his pace and further improving his action and technique, he soon prospered to become an all-time great.

ASHES
— SCORECARD —

Dennis Lillee

Name: Dennis Lillee

Born: 1949

Appearances: 29

High score: 73 n.o. (Lord's, 1975)

Batting average: 18.03

Best figures: 7-89 (The Oval, 1981)

Bowling average: 21.00

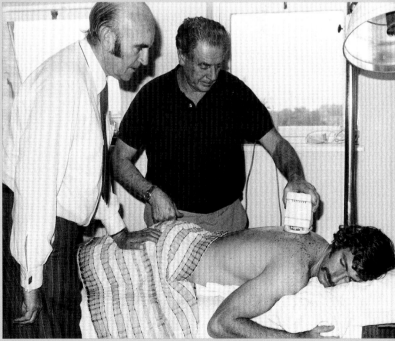

LEFT: For all Lillee's excellence, England had enough nous and quality to come through the 1972 series with a 2-2 draw and so retain the Ashes. Captain Ray Illingworth, ranked by many as England's best leader after Hutton, basked in the achievement on the Headingley balcony after victory in the fourth Test gave his side an unassailable 2-1 lead.

BELOW: Australia signed off in 1972 with a win, however, in the final rubber, recording a five-wicket victory at The Oval. England's John Hampshire was unimpressed with Rodney Marsh appealing for a stumping.

ABOVE: The consistently large crowds at The Oval reflected the interest garnered by a series between two well-matched and well-supported sides.

RIGHT: Prime Minister Edward Heath went to accommodating lengths to provide his autograph.

BELOW: Making moves in The Oval scoreboard were groundsman Robert Hilliard, 22, and his fiancée Sandra MacManson, who were enjoying a game of chess during a lull in the action.

RIGHT: A score of 16 for 1 and no sign of checkmate from the scoreboard grandmasters just yet.

143

144

The Aussies toasted the win in 1972 (left), with skipper Ian Chappell hitting the bubbly (above). There were to be plenty more champagne Ashes moments to come for this emerging team.

LEFT: The change in the balance of power between the two sides became clear during the 1974–75 series. Australia romped to a 4-1 victory, built on the bowling of Lillee and Thomson, the latter bouncing back to blistering form after being written off for two years. England suffered for the absence of Geoff Boycott who had withdrawn from Test cricket claiming stress and fatigue with touring. It was left to the likes of David Lloyd to try and withstand the twin assaults of the home side's frightening pace attack.

BELOW: Alan Knott was at his competitive best at the MCG, taking four catches in the drawn rubber.

Lillee (below) was at the peak of his powers and, with Thomson (right, in the pool), was a constant and notably painful thorn in England's side. Thomson had been dismissed in some quarters as a "beach bum" but proved to be a bowler of venomous intent – with the wickets to show for it.

LEFT: The four-match 1975 series in England had been hastily arranged for a number of reasons: to replace the cancelled series against the ostracized South Africans, to help England make amends for the Ashes loss six months earlier, and to exploit the buzz created by cricket's inaugural World Cup. In addition, Lillee and Thomson were big and entertaining draws; the former throws a towel over 12th man Gary Gilmour.

ABOVE: Tony Greig took over the England captaincy from Mike Denness, instilling some renewed purpose into the team, though the series was still lost 1-0. Greig surveyed the damage to the Headingley wicket that was caused by protestors campaigning for the release of armed robber George Davis. They dug holes over the pitch and poured oil over one end of the wicket, robbing England of the chance of victory, though rain struck in any case.

Australia Sent Packering

The Aussies returned to Heathrow full of smiles in 1977 but, plagued by splits over the WSC series, they slumped to a 3-0 defeat. They were led this time by Greg Chappell (centre, with David Hookes right, and Jeff Thomson left) after Chappell's brother Ian joined Kerry Packer's rival format.

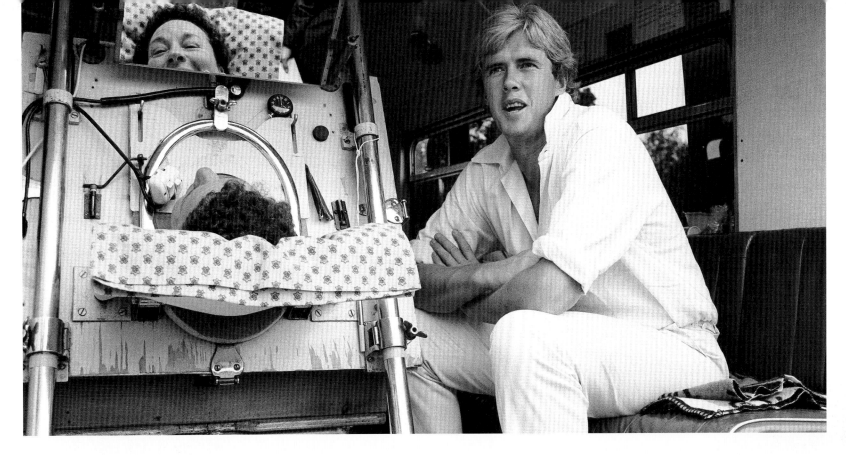

ABOVE: Kerry O'Keeffe chatted to cricket fan Margaret Dixon in her iron lung during the Australia v Rest of the World match at Arundel in August 1977.

BELOW: Doug Walters (right) and Len Pascoe wore their feelings on their shirts in a warm-up match at Hove in May, which was delayed by rain.

ABOVE: The Tavern crowd kept their spirits up with a bout of community singing as the rain fell during the second day's play of the Queen's Jubilee Test at Lord's.

RIGHT: England too had their own changes, and with Greig having been a prime mover in playing for and organizing Kerry Packer's venture, he was stripped of the England captaincy. Mike Brearley (second right) was called up as replacement.

Boycs is back: England had missed the dogged batting of Geoff Boycott and he was welcomed into the fold again at Trent Bridge. He responded with 107 in the first innings and carried his bat for 80 in the second as England won by seven wickets. Boycott then scored 191 at his home ground of Headingley – his 100th century – as England trounced the Aussies by an innings and 85 runs.

LEFT: Greig was still in the side but was skittled out for 11 by Thomson in the first innings at Nottingham.

BELOW: Derek Randall was an outstanding fielder – and made an impressive catch at Trent Bridge.

> "Aussies know only one way to play – to win."
>
> Ian Botham

156

The end of the decade saw England hand out a humbling 5-1 win in the 1978–79 series and the arrival of Ian Botham – the Ashes would never be quite the same again. In December 1979 (during a series without the Ashes up for grabs) he sat alongside a youthful David Gower, Bob Taylor, behind the lens, and Peter Willey.

> " *Aussies are big and empty,*
> *just like their country.*
>
> Ian Botham

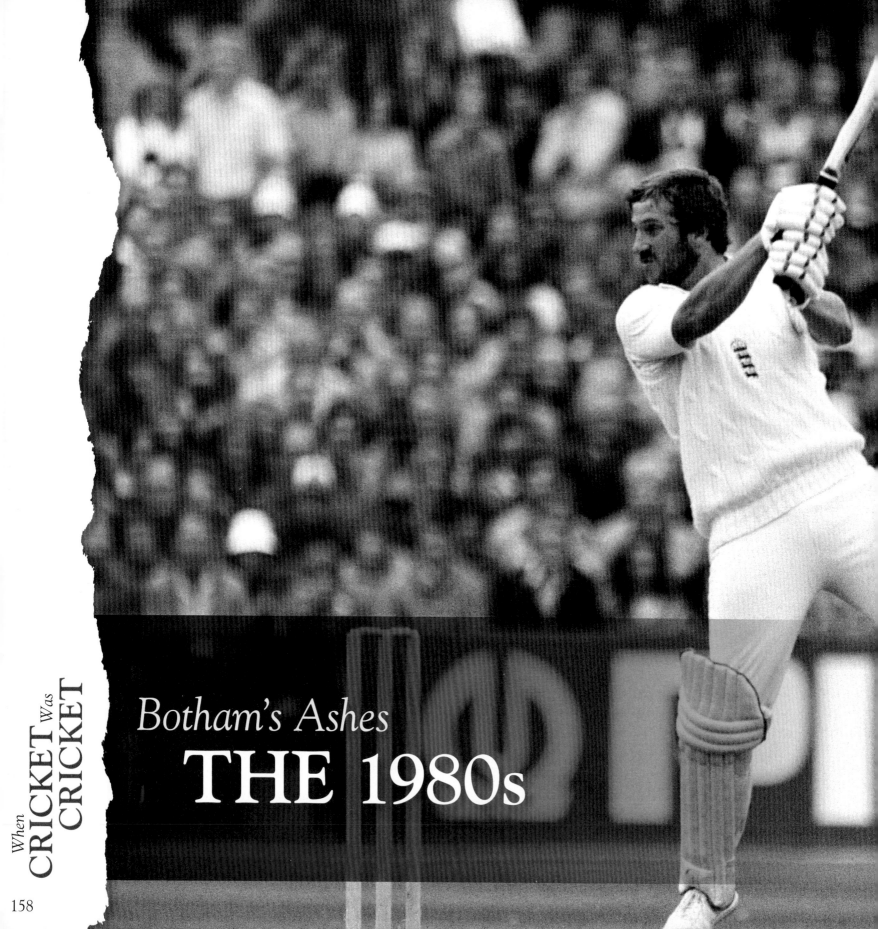

Botham's Ashes
THE 1980s

Hail the conquering hero. Ian Botham, the supreme star of the 1981 series, in typically swashbuckling form on day three of the fifth Test at Old Trafford.

1980 saw the 100th anniversary of the first Test to be played in England against Australia. While the original in 1880 took place at The Oval, the centenary game was hosted by Lord's and ended in a draw.

Ashes competition proper resumed with the 1981 summer series in England. It was to become one of the best in the history not just of the Ashes but cricket as a whole, with a series of unforgettable games and a dramatic England recovery, inspired by the heroic Ian Botham. His match-winning displays at Headingley (in tandem with a seemingly possessed Bob Willis), and then at Edgbaston, turned a series that seemed to be heading inexorably in Australia's favour and provided a modern English cricketing hero cast in the "boy's own" mould.

The Aussies gained revenge in 1982–83 but it was the last hurrah for key members of the side, including Dennis Lillee and Greg Chappell. For the return in 1985, England retrieved the urn with a 3-1 series victory under the captaincy of the elegant David Gower. This was followed by a 2-1 win in 1986–87, but this was to be the last taste of English victory for almost a generation: Australia's 4-0 victory on English soil in 1989 was a foretaste of domination by one of the greatest and most consistent sides in cricket history.

1981 – Guy the Thriller

The 1981 series began in ignominious fashion for England. The visitors took a 1-0 lead after a four-wicket victory in the first Test at Trent Bridge. A low-scoring game on a tricky pitch for batting saw the Aussies require just 132 runs in their second innings, which they duly secured with four wickets to spare.

   The defeat heaped pressure on England's beleaguered skipper, Ian Botham. Having lost two series to the West Indies – the pre-eminent side of the era – Botham was given only partial backing by the England selectors, with a rolling, game-by-game deal to lead his side through the Ashes series. A draw in the second Test at Lord's did little to alleviate the burden on Botham's broad shoulders, and after suffering a pair – including a golden duck in the second innings – he resigned.

ABOVE: Dennis Lillee couldn't bring himself to look as Australia and England laboured to a draw in an ill-tempered match at Lord's.

The second Test was as interesting for what took place off the pitch as on it. After his second duck of the match, soon-to-be-deposed captain Botham trudged back to the pavilion in deafening silence from the MCC members, who studied their papers or even turned their backs as Botham made the walk past them and up the steps.

On the second day, some among the crowd reacted with fury when a misunderstanding between the umpires and the Test and County Cricket Board (TCCB) meant an extra hour of play was lost to bad light even though the sun was shining. Spectators rained down cushions onto the pitch. What looked like the start of an ugly incident was turned when Godfrey Evans, former England wicket-keeping great, emerged onto the balcony clutching a gin and tonic. He joked with the crowd, and in avoiding any hits from the flying cushions without spilling a drop of his tipple got the spectators laughing and calmed the situation.

ABOVE: England's misery appeared to be resulting in another dispiriting defeat when they followed on in their second innings in the third Test at Headingley. Chasing a target of 401 in the first innings, the home side were skittled out for just 174 and in the follow on, when David Gower was caught by Alan Border off the bowling of Terry Alderman, a heavy defeat was all but inevitable. The England players checked out of their hotel, and at odds of 500/1, some of the Australians reputedly could not resist a cheeky if outlandish wager on the home side.

Cue Ian Botham. With an unforgettable knock of 149 (ably assisted by Graham Dilley), Botham carried his bat and gave England an unlikely if slim hope.

"The most magnificent spell of sustained hostile bowling it has ever been my privilege to witness."

– Ian Botham, on Bob Willis' second innings performance

BELOW: Got him! Bob Willis celebrates as Geoff Lawson is caught by Bob Taylor for just one as the England paceman propelled his team towards one of the most remarkable comeback victories in cricket history. Botham's aggregate of 199 runs and seven wickets for 109 was fundamental to the win, but Willis bowled with a near-demonic intensity to take eight second innings wickets for just 43 runs and so demolish Australia's reply.

"It was pure village green stuff."

Mike Brearley on the Headingley fightback

England players and fans celebrate an extraordinary Ashes triumph at Headingley.

British Beefy

"Beefy", "Guy", "Both" – Ian Botham's brawny, macho nicknames revealed much about the great man's appeal as a true cricketing hero. While many Aussies love to label English players as "whingeing Poms" who lack the fight and the sheer guts to compete in top-level sport, they had no room for mockery with Botham. A born winner if ever there was, he could grab a game by the scruff of its neck and turn adversity into triumph. It stemmed from a combination of fierce competitiveness, no little bravado and an uncommon all-round talent.

The Ashes provided Botham with a fitting stage. While he struggled as captain, his abilities as a right-hand bat, right-arm fast-medium bowler and accomplished fielder gave him the attributes to impose his skill and will on matches.

He made his Ashes debut against the Aussies in 1977 and had an immediate impact with a "five-for". In the 1981 series it was a topsy-turvy time for Botham. He was relieved of the captaincy, to be replaced by the expert in man-management, Mike Brearley. While he still denies that the change freed him from any supposed shackling effect of leadership, Botham the all-round cricketing genius flourished once more. He was not alone in turning the series around, but no English cricketer before or since was able to make such a dramatic, thrilling and memorable individual mark.

Take that: Botham strikes out in a 1985 one-day international against the old enemy.

MAN OF THE
– ERA –

Sir Ian Botham

Out on the fundraising trail, this time in a £1-a-bowl charity session at Gateshead Stadium in July 1986. Botham had an eventful, often acrimonious relationship with the media, in particular the press, but amid all the tabloid scandal he was also a willing columnist. In retirement from playing, Botham has become a forthright but accomplished commentator.

SCOREBOARD

AUSTRALIA. First innings: 401 for nine dec. (Dyson 102, Hughes 89, Yallop 58; Botham six for 95).

Second innings
Dyson, c Taylor, b Willis 34
Wood, c Taylor, b Botham 10
Chappell, c Taylor, b Willis 8
Hughes, c Botham, b Willis 0
Yallop, c Gatting, b Willis 0
Border, b Old 0
Marsh, c Dilley, b Willis 4
Bright, b Willis 19
Lawson, c Taylor, b Willis 1
Lillee, c Gatting, b Willis 17
Alderman, not out 0
Extras (lb3, w1, nb14) 18
Total 111
Fall: 1-13, 2-56, 3-58, 4-58, 5-65, 6-68, 7-74, 8-75, 9-110.
Bowling: Botham 7-3-14-1; Dilley 2-0-11-0; Willis 15. 1-3-43-8; Old 9-1-21-1; Willey 3-1-4-0.

ENGLAND. First innings: 174 Second innings: 356 (Botham 149 not Dilley 56; Alderman 6-135).

ASHES
— SCORECARD —

Sir Ian Botham

Name: Ian Botham

Born: 1955

Appearances: 36

High score: 149 n.o. (Headingley, 1981)

Batting average: 29.35

Best figures: 6-78 (Perth, 1979)*

Bowling average: 27.66

(* The Ashes were not at stake in the 1979–80 three-match series)

ABOVE: Seeing is believing: the scoreboard told the tale of Botham and Willis' remarkable performances.

LEFT: Botham became famous for his epic charity walks. In 1987 in Belfast, he was joined by snooker champion Alex "Hurricane" Higgins.

ABOVE: Lightning really did strike twice when Ian Botham produced another match-winning display against all the odds, this time with one of the greatest bowling performances in Ashes history, at Edgbaston.

RIGHT: England's players celebrated after another extraordinary victory, this time in the fourth Test at Birmingham – and with Botham once again the centre of attention.

The wicket at Birmingham was supposed to be high scoring – Australia's skipper Kim Hughes reckoned it might produce 900 runs – but instead it was a bowler's delight. England were rolled over for 189 before Australia responded with 258. England's modest 219 in their second innings left the visitors needing just 151 to regain the series lead.

In stepped Botham. With a blistering spell of devastating bowling, he ripped through the Aussie's middle order and scythed through five wickets for just 11 runs, to give England a 2-1 series lead.

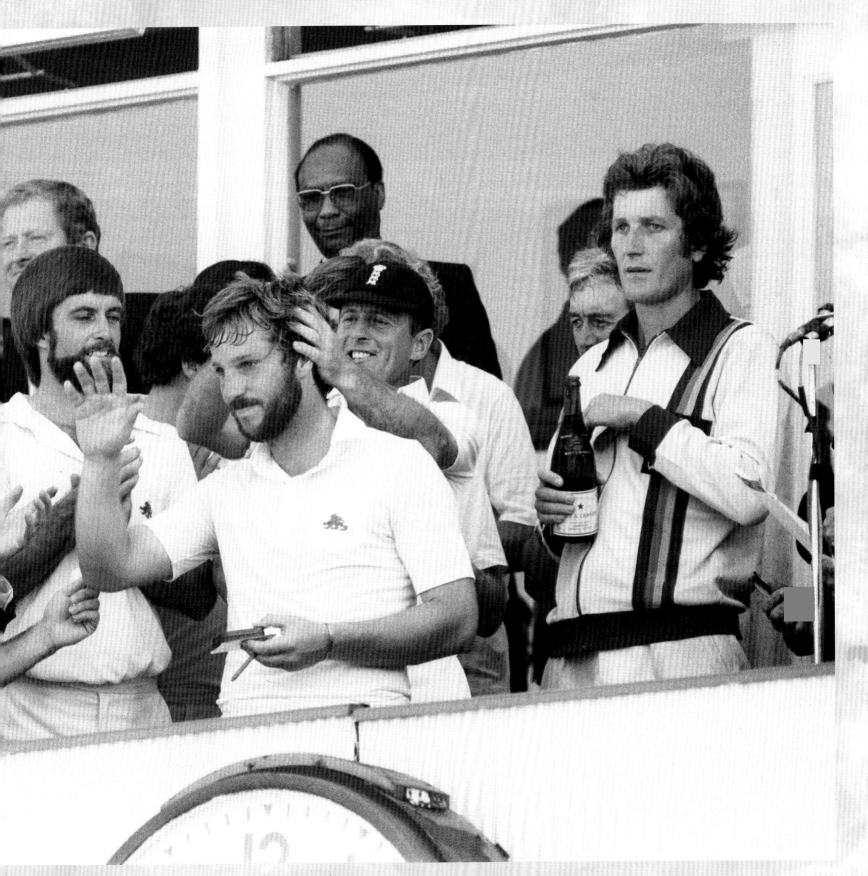

It's that man again. Botham leapt to take a great catch and remove John Dyson for a duck from the bowling of Willis, as England dismissed Australia for 130 in their first innings at Old Trafford. With a first innings lead of 101, England were in good shape in the second innings but collapsed to 104 for 5. Botham yet again rescued the situation and, in tandem with Chris Tavaré, rallied the side with a 149-run partnership. Botham harvested 118 runs, providing the mainstay of a lead that Australia could not overcome, despite a brave second innings total of 402. England won by 103 runs and, with this victory, won the Ashes.

> *He has a degree in people.*
>
> Aussie fast bowler Rodney
> Hogg on Brearley

ABOVE: Alan Border looks suitably disgruntled as two fans run onto the wicket to remove the bails at Old Trafford.

LEFT: Mike Brearley, pictured second left with the Duke of Edinburgh, was the captain whose superb leadership skills underpinned England's success in the 1981 series. A well-educated man with a first in Classics from his time at Cambridge, Brearley went on to carve out a subsequent career as a leading psychoanalyst.

With the series won by the time of the final Test at The Oval, England fans were in flag-waving, triumphant mood.

After gaining a first innings lead (despite England's Geoffrey Boycott scoring 137 in a knock that boasted just three boundaries), Australia set the hosts a total of 383 on the final day. But the visitors' attempts to win the match and narrow the series deficit were, like this appeal, in vain.

Handshakes all round after the final Test ended in a draw.
Man of the Match Dennis Lillee joined Man of the Series Ian
Botham as Ashes hostilities abated for another year.

Australia fought back in the 1982–83 series to reclaim the Ashes for the first time in eight years, but England rallied in 1985 on home turf. The Aussies were now skippered by Allan Border (right), who succeeded Kim Hughes (after the latter's tearful resignation in the aftermath of a thrashing by the all-conquering West Indies), and, in addition, the returning Greg Chappell.

Border was charged with revitalizing a dispirited Australian outfit to restore both morale and form. It was a tough task, and did not bring immediate dividends, but Border was to play a key role in the emergence of what became a dominant Aussie side.

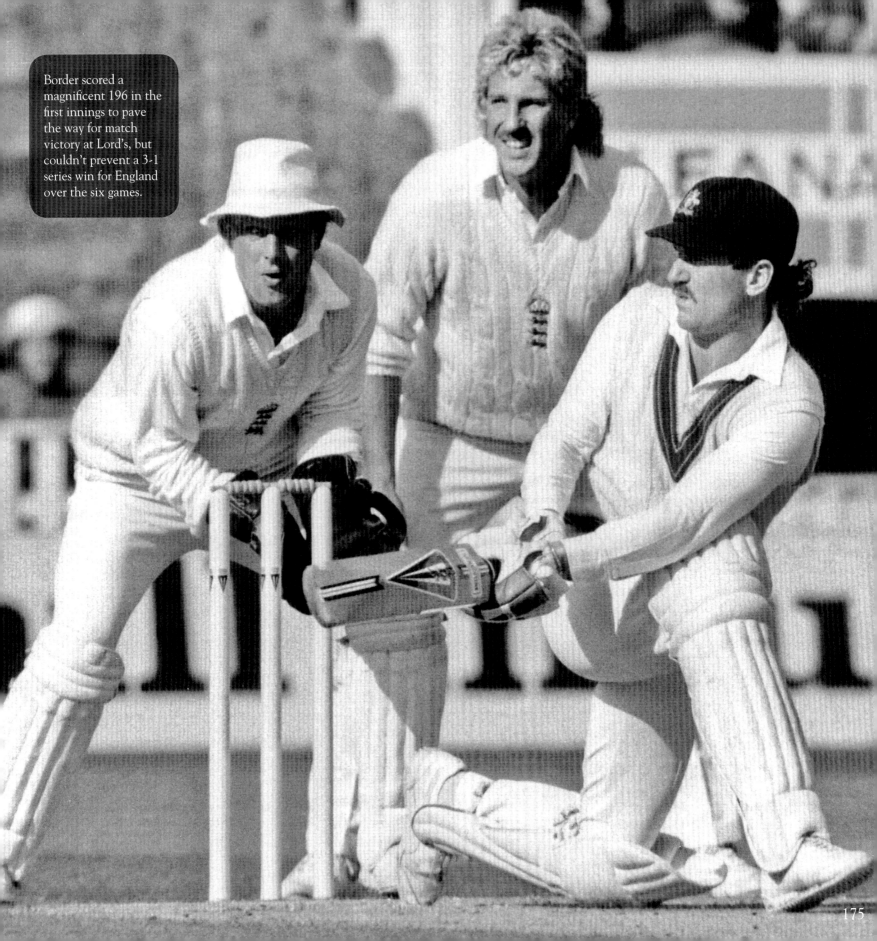

Border scored a magnificent 196 in the first innings to pave the way for match victory at Lord's, but couldn't prevent a 3-1 series win for England over the six games.

Rain at Edgbaston forced spectators and players to take cover.

LEFT: Captain David Gower, the consummate elegant stroke-maker in the England side, scored a wonderful 166 in the third Test at Trent Bridge.

BELOW: Gower (left) in England's slip cordon at Lord's in 1985.

England retained the Ashes with another series win in Australia in 1986–87, but it was to be a long time coming before the country held sway in the old rivalry again. Australia's 4-0 series win in 1989 was a comprehensive demonstration of the team's all-round quality, and heralded a long fallow period for England, despite the continuing best efforts of Ian Botham.

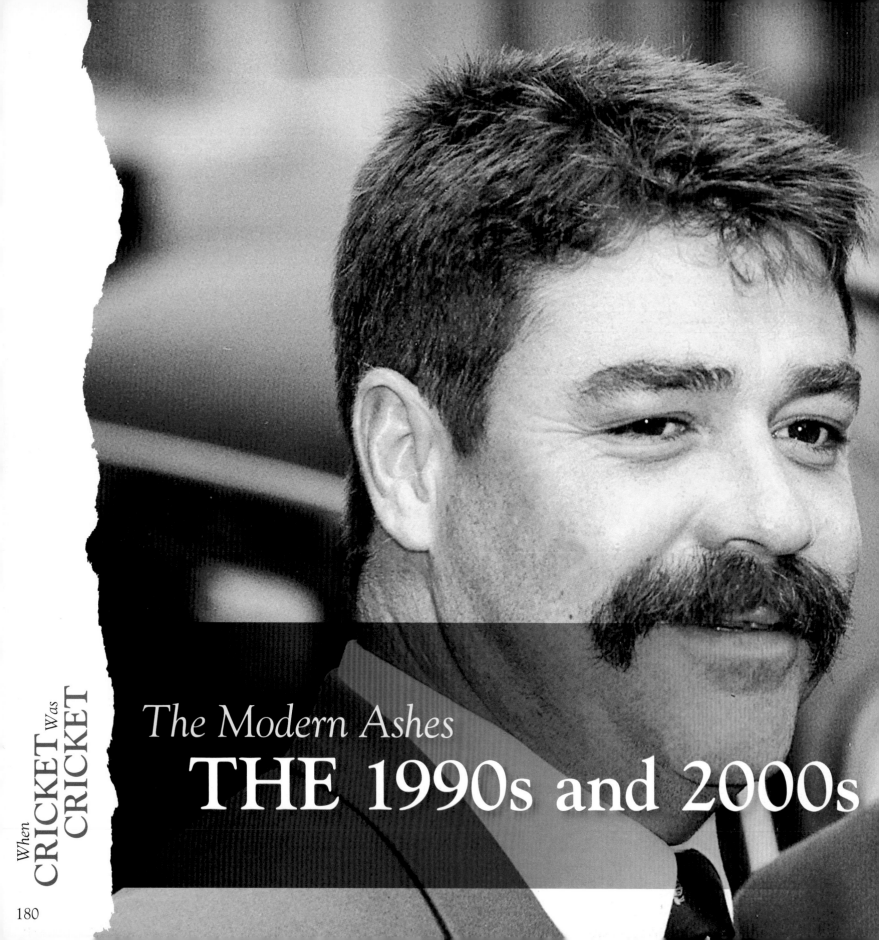

When CRICKET *Was* CRICKET

The Modern Ashes
THE 1990s and 2000s

Australia's rise to the pinnacle of world cricket entailed Ashes supremacy as well. Having retained the urn with a 3-0 win in 1990–91, the Aussies returned in 1993 and recorded a handsome 4-1 victory. With English cricket beleaguered and in a prolonged trough, the rivalry took on a lopsided nature: the mother country was not to enjoy Ashes success for another 12 years.

Allan Border, one of the main architects of the Aussie revival, retired in 1994, but there was no let-up in success for his erstwhile team-mates. Mark Taylor took over the captaincy and, having made 839 Test runs on his first tour of England in 1989, maintained the overall level of superiority. The Australians won 3-1 in 1994–95, and while England narrowed the gap to 3-2 in 1997 under Michael Atherton's leadership, comprehensive victories in 1998–99, 2001 and 2002–03 extended Australia's winning streak to eight successive series. England finally took the urn in a memorable series in 2005.

All smiles and all moustaches as David Boon (left) and Merv Hughes (right) arrive for the Ashes battle, which recommenced in April 1993.

When CRICKET *was* CRICKET

Warning Sign

One of the principal tormentors of England during the long years of Aussie Ashes domination, Shane Warne is a sunshine-haired, charismatic, rebellious, occasionally troublesome but more frequently brilliant bowler, and one of the finest players in cricket history. He rediscovered and restored the seemingly lost art of leg spin, was placed in *Wisden*'s list of the five best cricketers of the 20th century, and his reputation was, in large part, forged by his match-winning exploits against England.

Warne announced his talent to the world with his first Ashes over, reaping the wicket of Mike Gatting, who had been left utterly flummoxed by a ball that turned so wickedly that it seemed to defy the laws of physics. Warne would go on to incur further havoc through English batting orders; he was a nemesis to opponents who invariably could not cope with the bowler's supreme skill, craft and artistry. Even at the end of his career he was still harvesting English wickets with alacrity, taking 40 in 2005 and ending with a record-setting 195 by 2007. He was no slouch with the bat, either, and his record for scoring more Test runs (3,154 of them) without reaching a century than any other player was nearly broken when he scored 90 at Old Trafford in 2005.

Given his rambunctious reputation and a tendency to get caught up in tabloid scandal, Warne was an eye-catching performer who was the inevitable focus of much mickey-taking and less savoury attention from some England fans. But alongside the mockery there was huge respect for one of the great players of the modern or any era. Warne was a genius, and true cricket supporters readily recognized and conferred that distinction.

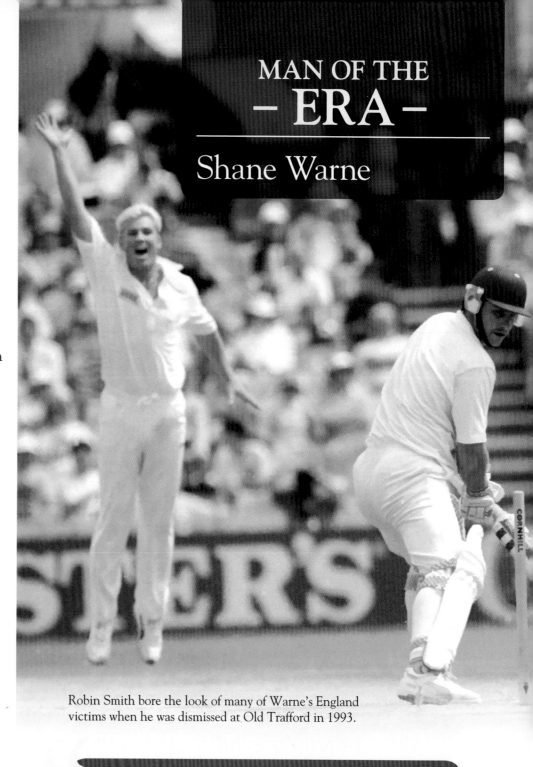

MAN OF THE
– ERA –

Shane Warne

Robin Smith bore the look of many of Warne's England victims when he was dismissed at Old Trafford in 1993.

400 wickets is 400 more than I thought I'd get.

– Shane Warne

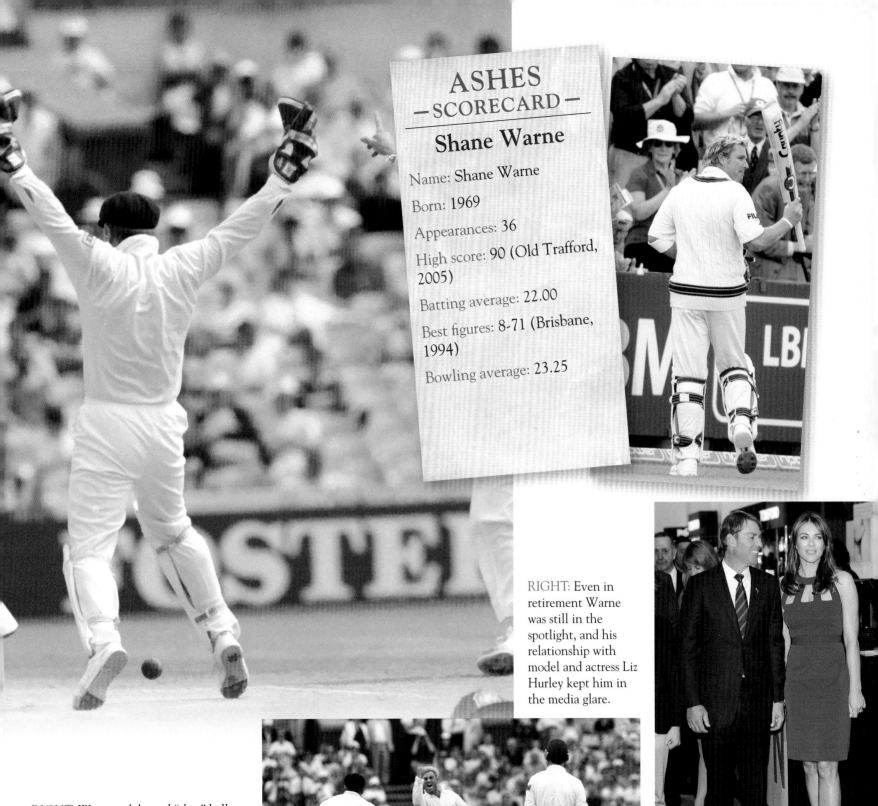

ASHES
— SCORECARD —
Shane Warne

Name: Shane Warne

Born: 1969

Appearances: 36

High score: 90 (Old Trafford, 2005)

Batting average: 22.00

Best figures: 8-71 (Brisbane, 1994)

Bowling average: 23.25

RIGHT: Even in retirement Warne was still in the spotlight, and his relationship with model and actress Liz Hurley kept him in the media glare.

RIGHT: Warne celebrated "that" ball against Mike Gatting in 1993. The late cricket journalist and commentator Christopher Martin-Jenkins wrote in the *Daily Telegraph* that it "spun back with the speed of a cobra".

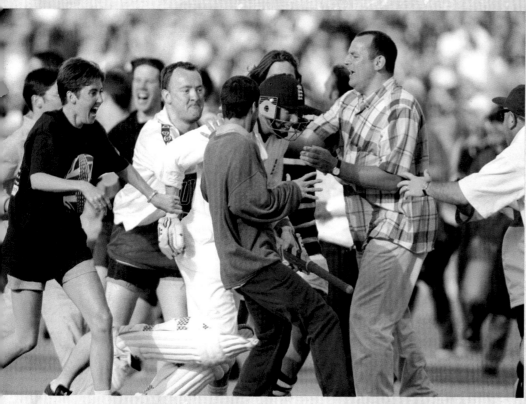

ABOVE: Michael Atherton is mobbed after England's unexpected but very welcome nine-wicket win at Edgbaston in 1997. Atherton had taken over the England captaincy from Graham Gooch, to fulfil a destiny his Mancunian friends had predicted for him when he was a young player. They nicknamed him "FEC" for Future England Captain, though there are stories that the "E" stood for educated and the "F" and "C" for something altogether less complimentary.

Whatever the truth, he was handed a huge burden when he was appointed to try and revive a team stuck in the doldrums. England's poor form had pushed them further and further down the rankings. While Atherton may not have delivered much in the way of Ashes series victories, he gave England purpose and resolve in some very testing circumstances.

RIGHT: The jubilant crowd at Edgbaston reflected a new sense of optimism among England fans. But could it be sustained?

ABOVE: The answer came in the third Test at Old Trafford, where a brilliant 6 for 48 from Warne helped Australia towards a thumping 268-run win. Thereafter, the tourists established a winning 3-1 series lead.

LEFT: Steve Waugh was the captain-in-waiting in 1997, and his near flawless performances at the crease played a large part in Australia's long period of domination. His two centuries at Old Trafford were a prime example of his technique, coolness and unflappable determination.

ABOVE: Andy Caddick appealed at Trent Bridge in the fifth Test of 1997 but it was, ultimately, to no avail: Australia won by 264 runs.

> *If we can get on top early, we can open up some old scars.*
>
> – Steve Waugh

LEFT: Steve Waugh had taken over the Australian captaincy and lifted a crystal replica of the Ashes urn after his side defeated England at The Oval, and thus retained the Ashes with a 4-1 series win in 2001.

BELOW: Fast bowler Brett Lee was one of the new young stars of the Aussie side, an example of the conveyor belt of talent that maintained his country's rule as cricket kings.

Another Ashes Test, another Australian celebration. Lord's was something of a graveyard for England against Australia, and the tourists' eight-wicket win in 2001 was yet further confirmation of the standing between the two great rivals. Led by Nasser Hussain, England went into the series with improved expectations after good wins against the West Indies and Pakistan, but, hit by injuries, his team had little answer to the remorseless excellence of the supreme Australian outfit. Once the Australians turned the screw, England were comfortably contained.

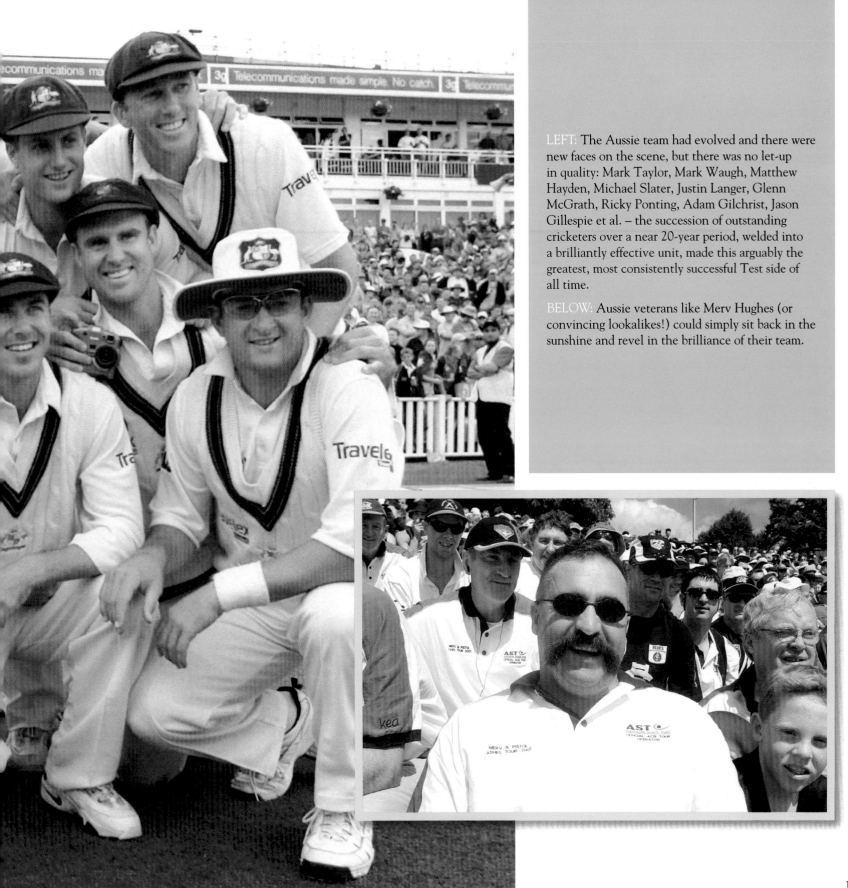

LEFT: The Aussie team had evolved and there were new faces on the scene, but there was no let-up in quality: Mark Taylor, Mark Waugh, Matthew Hayden, Michael Slater, Justin Langer, Glenn McGrath, Ricky Ponting, Adam Gilchrist, Jason Gillespie et al. – the succession of outstanding cricketers over a near 20-year period, welded into a brilliantly effective unit, made this arguably the greatest, most consistently successful Test side of all time.

BELOW: Aussie veterans like Merv Hughes (or convincing lookalikes!) could simply sit back in the sunshine and revel in the brilliance of their team.

The Old Country Strikes Back

It had been a long time coming – but England's campaign to regain the Ashes in 2005 was one of the most epic sporting contests of the modern era. Finally able to compete with, match and even surpass the Aussie's talent and hitherto unquenchable will-to-win, this was an England side, brilliantly led by Michael Vaughan (left), which was determined that, this time, there were to be no more disappointments, no more hard-luck stories.

After the familiar defeat at Lord's in the first Test, English confidence was jolted, but soon rallied at Edgbaston after the home side won one of the most thrilling and pulsating matches in Ashes or any Test history. With just two wickets remaining, Australia's valiant attempt to bat out the fourth and final day and then eke out the runs to record an unlikely victory were dashed when Brett Lee and Michael Kasprowicz's heroic last stand was ended with only two runs to spare – the closest winning margin in Ashes history.

ABOVE: Frustration for Simon Jones at the third Test at Old Trafford, but the Welshman's reverse swing was a prime weapon in the English armoury, and his 18 wickets over four matches were a crucial contribution to the cause.

RIGHT: If the result at Edgbaston was a key turning point in the series, so too was the absence of brilliant Aussie paceman Glenn McGrath (left, with Jason Gillespie), one of the greatest fast bowlers in cricket history. McGrath was injured after stepping on a ball in practice and tearing his ankle ligaments. It ruled him out for the match and contributed to a series display that was less potent than his usual magnificent best. For so many years, McGrath's impeccable line, length and consistency had made him the bête noire of English batsmen. His absence or restricted effectiveness in key matches in 2005 proved decisive.

By the time this epic series reached its dramatic conclusion at The Oval, England had established a narrow 2-1 lead, thanks to a three-wicket victory in Nottingham following the draw at Old Trafford. All England required was another draw to ensure they would claim the Ashes for the first time in 16 long, dispiriting years. "All" – against a magnificent Australian side that refused to countenance defeat – the task was monumental.

Roared on by an expectant, feverish crowd, England established a wafer-thin six-run first innings lead, built on a terrific partnership between centurion Andrew Strauss and Andrew Flintoff. But in the second innings, when Ricky Ponting caught Paul Collingwood off Shane Warne's spin (below), it ratcheted up the tension to almost unbearable levels. England were nearly home, but not quite there, just yet …

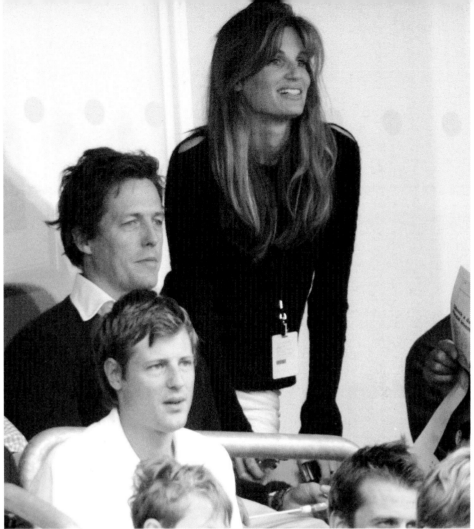

The thrilling denouement to the 2005 series brought out the celebs to the more salubrious seats at The Oval, including actor Hugh Grant, Jemima Khan and Zac Goldsmith (above) …

… as well as Lesley Garrett, former PM John Major, Tessa Jowell and Sir Trevor McDonald (below).

LEFT: Skipper Ricky Ponting was frustrated by the conditions that resulted in a stop–start nature to The Oval Test, but was also questioned for the decision of his batsmen to take the bad light when offered.

RIGHT: Blood came from the neck of Andrew Strauss after he was hit by a ball from Brett Lee.

As the tension increased, it seemed the whole nation was tuning in to see if England could do it. At The Oval – or just outside it – fans clambered onto the roofs of nearby buildings to sneak a peak at the gripping action (above), while at Canary Wharf office workers took time out to watch the action on a giant screen (left). It was all very reminiscent of 1953.

England's defence of their series lead was built on Andrew Strauss' century in the first innings and a brilliant debut Test century from Kevin Pietersen in their second innings. After surviving a couple of early scares, including being dropped by Warne, the South African-born-and-raised Pietersen produced an innings that stirred memories of Botham at Headingley in 1981. With the staunch assistance of, first, Paul Collingwood and then Ashley Giles, Pietersen's 158 ensured that, from an English perspective, the Ashes would be coming home.

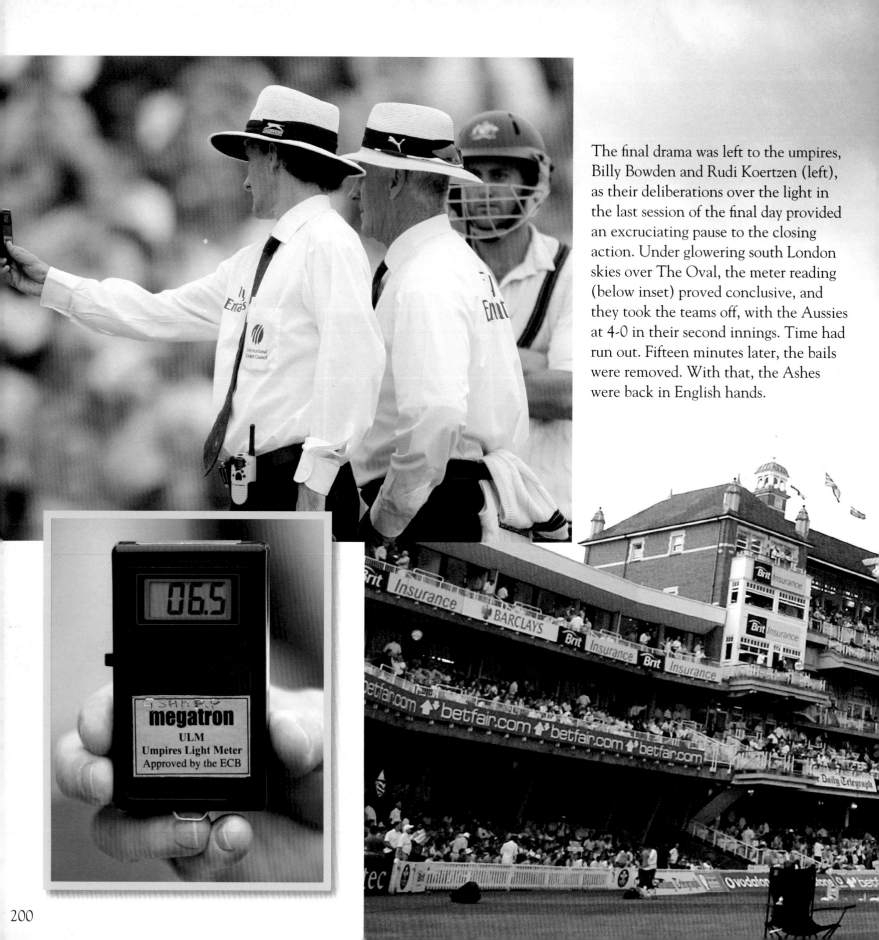

The final drama was left to the umpires, Billy Bowden and Rudi Koertzen (left), as their deliberations over the light in the last session of the final day provided an excruciating pause to the closing action. Under glowering south London skies over The Oval, the meter reading (below inset) proved conclusive, and they took the teams off, with the Aussies at 4-0 in their second innings. Time had run out. Fifteen minutes later, the bails were removed. With that, the Ashes were back in English hands.

Victory at last

203

An aerial view over Trafalgar Square, showing just a part of the vast crowd that greeted the England side in their victory parade on 13th September 2005. The series victory did more than register a win over Australia – it reinvigorated an English game that had seemed to be in terminal decline, and restored the sport to the nation's heart.

Ashes Cheers

> *Journalist: Have you had anything to eat?*
> *Flintoff: Yes. A cigar.*
>
> conversation amid the Ashes celebrations

ABOVE: England had many cricketing heroes that glorious summer of 2005, but none were as influential, and certainly none more charismatic, as Andrew Flintoff. His feats with bat and ball during his career, notably in meetings with the old adversaries, cast him in the mould of an Ian Botham for a new generation – and created new tales to add to the ever-growing legends of the Ashes.

LEFT: Matthew Hoggard, a vital member of England's pace attack, cradled both Ashes urn and beer bottle in the dressing room.

England ascendant: Captain Andrew Strauss lifts the Ashes in 2009. Australia had won the urn back with a devastating 5-0 whitewash in 2006–07, but a win on home soil two years later and then a comprehensive 3-1 down under, suggested the balance of power was at last shifting England's way. The Ashes, as history has shown, however, will often spring surprises …

Acknowledgements

Thanks to Vito Inglese, Dave Scripps and all at Mirrorpix, the team at Haynes, Paul Moreton, Kevin Gardner, Elizabeth Stone and Rebecca Ellis.

Very special thanks to Richard Havers.

This book relies on a host of exemplary sources and references, in particular the following:

Wisden on the Ashes, ed. Steven Lynch (John Wisden & Co., 2009)
Head On: The Autobiography, Ian Botham (Ebury Press, 2007)
Phoenix from the Ashes, Mike Brearley (Hodder & Stoughton, 1982)
Cricinfo.com
BBC
Daily Mirror
Heinz Archive at the History of Advertising Trust